HANDS-ON BASIC

FOR THE IBM® PERSONAL COMPUTER

Joyce O. Devine

HANDS-ON BASIC
FOR THE IBM® PERSONAL COMPUTER

HERBERT PECKHAM

A Computer Literacy™ BOOK

McGRAW-HILL BOOK COMPANY

NEW YORK ST. LOUIS SAN FRANCISCO AUCKLAND
BOGOTÁ HAMBURG JOHANNESBURG LONDON MADRID
MEXICO MONTREAL NEW DELHI PANAMA PARIS
SÃO PAULO SINGAPORE SIDNEY TOKYO TORONTO

HANDS-ON BASIC: For the IBM® Personal Computer

234567890 HALHAL 89876543

ISBN 0-07-049178-X

LIBRARY OF CONGRESS CATALOG CARD NUMBER: 82-81497

This book was set in Patina and Eras using the TEX composition system.
The editor was Charles E. Stewart; the production supervisor was John Mancia.
The designer was Paul Quin.
Halliday Lithograph Corporation was printer and binder.

CONTENTS

PREFACE

This book is a modification of an earlier work by the author that was also published by McGraw-Hill Book Company. That book, entitled *BASIC: A Hands-on Method,* introduces students to BASIC on a number of different timesharing computers. This earlier material has been revised and modified to be used specifically on the personal computer manufactured by the International Business Machines Corporation. Since the motivation and ideas that lead to the original work are equally valid with respect to the IBM Personal Computer, they bear repeating in this book.

Two characteristics of most BASIC programming texts on the market are very objectionable. First, almost all quickly begin to use mathematics at a level that excludes the vast majority of those we are most interested in, many of whom can rely on introductory algebra (very dimly remembered) but who need to learn how to program in BASIC. The second objection is that generally nothing in the structure of the texts requires the reader to spend much (if any) time on the computer. Students typically try to study programming like any other subject and do not feel the need to experiment with and execute programs on the computer. This text's main thesis is that more traditional text material should be preceded by a good deal of time experimenting with the language on the computer. The experience to date validates the idea that people work through the material more rapidly and effectively with this initial exposure to BASIC on the computer.

Most textbooks are used in a classroom environment as part of the formal educational system. Certainly, many people will learn how to program in this traditional setting. However, the sales of personal computers will touch all parts of our society. This means that the usual concept of a "student" must be changed dramatically.

This text has been designed to be useful to anyone (whether part of the educational system or not) who wants to learn how to program the IBM Personal Computer.

The reader will note immediately that the structure of this book is quite different from that of most texts on the market. Each chapter begins with a statement of the objectives for that chapter. Then you are guided through a set of exercises that let you experiment with the characteristics of BASIC and see the language in action. Once you have acquired a "feel" for BASIC, you can profitably proceed to a more traditional treatment of the concepts. The mathematics level has intentionally been kept very low. People with more advanced mathematics skills can learn to use these on the computer on their own. However, if the mathematics level in the text were set too high, the majority of beginners would become discouraged in the first few chapters. At the level presented, nearly everyone should be able to work through the material without getting "hung up" by the mathematics. The reader must have access to an IBM Personal Computer to use this book.

The text is organized into twelve chapters plus two appendices. Each chapter forms a module of instruction that should require about one or two hours on the computer and perhaps one or two hours studying the text. Review tests are provided at the end of each chapter, enabling the reader to see if the objectives have been mastered.

The book can be used in several different ways. First, and probably most important, it can be used with no supervision as a self-study text. This format has also been used very effectively in an open-entry, open-exit, self-paced course. If desired, the material can be presented in a traditional lecture format.

People at any level from junior high through graduate school should be able to use the material effectively. The goal is to provide programming skills in BASIC as rapidly and effectively as possible. As indicated above, no mathematics past introductory algebra is required, and the algebra used is mainly formula evaluation. More mathematical ability is nice but unnecessary.

Two documents furnished with the IBM Personal Computer have a bearing on the content and style of this book. First, there is the reference manual entitled *BASIC* that has all the specifications and capabilities of BASIC as implemented on the IBM Personal

Computer. Second, the *DOS* reference manual describes some additional capabilities of the IBM Personal Computer that will be used in this text.

This book is written for an IBM Personal Computer with the Color/Graphics Monitor Adapter, at least one disk drive, the Disk Operating System (DOS) diskette and either a black and white monitor/television set or a color monitor/television set. With the exception of Chapter 4 and a few examples and problems which require graphics statements, the book may be used with the IBM Monochrome Display.

ACKNOWLEDGMENTS

The International Business Machines Corporation and Computerland of San Jose, California provided generous assistance in the production of this book. Particular thanks are due to Wade Ellis, Jr. and Edward Lodi of the Computer Tutors of San Jose, California who assisted in revising the original textbook for the IBM Personal Computer and in typesetting the material in TEX.

The errors that remain are, of course, due to me. Comments or suggestions for improvement of this book will be appreciated.

Herbert D. Peckham

CHAPTER 1

INTRODUCTION TO COMPUTERS AND BASIC

Computers are now a common part of our lives. We may not see them, but they are there, involved in some way in most of our daily activities. Businesses of all sizes, educational institutions, various branches of government—none would be able to handle the bewildering quantity of information that seems to characterize our society except for computers. Only in recent years has the routine use of computers become a significant part of everyday activities. As the price of computers continues to drop, this trend will surely continue. More and more people will need to know how to use computers if they are to participate fully in our society.

What is BASIC?

You are about to embark upon the study of a computer language called BASIC. BASIC is a very specialized language designed to permit you and the computer to understand and communicate with one another. This language is not complicated and is certainly much easier to learn than a spoken language such as Spanish or French. Even so, BASIC does have a simple vocabulary consisting of a few words, a grammatical structure, and rules of use just like any other language. Your main tasks will be to learn the vocabulary of BASIC, become familiar with its rules of grammar, and begin to see how the language permits you to use the computer to do what you want. The level of mathematics involved has intentionally been kept very low. Therefore if you feel a bit rusty in your mathematical skills, don't be too concerned. As we proceed through BASIC, you will have an opportunity to brush up on some elementary mathematics.

A very effective way to learn about anything is to observe details and characteristics while performing a task: the "discovery" method. This is the strategy that will be used in this book. You will be asked to begin each chapter with a session on the computer. After following the directions and watching closely what the computer does in response to your instructions, you will begin to acquire a "feel" for BASIC. Once you have this type of understanding, you can proceed more profitably to study written material that summarizes what you have learned. Thus, the directed exercise on the computer is a key part of learning about BASIC as presented in this book.

Where Did BASIC Originate?

The original version of BASIC was designed and written at Dartmouth College under the direction of Professors John G. Kemeny and Thomas E. Kurtz. In September 1963 work began on a project to create a programming language written from the user's point of view. A very interesting sidelight was that much of the actual programming on the project was done by undergraduate students at Dartmouth. The birthday of BASIC is May 1, 1964.

The success of this pioneering effort at Dartmouth soon attracted national attention, and very quickly other institutions became interested. The rest is history. Today nearly every time-sharing computer supports some version of the BASIC language. The enhanced versions of the BASIC language have increased significantly the power and capability of the language over its early versions.

The most recent development is the use of BASIC on small, inexpensive personal computers. BASICA for the IBM Personal Computer, the language presented in this book, is a powerful and flexible enhanced version of BASIC. What started as a project at a single college is now an established part of the computer industry throughout the world.

How To Use This Book

Each chapter begins with a brief statement of the objectives. These should be studied carefully so you can get a clear picture of precisely what is to be done. (It's nice to know where you're going!) When asked, you should record the computer output in the space provided. Occasionally you will be asked to answer questions. The purpose of this activity is to lead you through the ideas involved and let you see BASIC working. It is important that you try to think about what will happen in situations that will be set up. This is an active relationship between you and the computer and should not be slighted. Whether or not your answers are correct is not important. The important thing is that you think carefully about the questions and try to answer. Time spent in this activity will save you time later on.

Following the discovery exercises in each chapter, a complete discussion is given to cover all the objectives a second time. Since you will have already seen the ideas and concepts in action on the computer, your study of this material will be much easier and more profitable.

Typical programs are included in each chapter. These are discussed in great detail to point out how elements of programming are pulled together to produce a BASIC program.

Each chapter past Chapter 5 has a collection of problems. You should plan to work enough problems to satisfy yourself that you can write programs at the level appropriate to each chapter. Solutions to the odd-numbered problems are at the end of the book.

Finally, each chapter (except the first) has a practice test. The purpose of this test is to review your understanding of the material and point out any areas that need further study. The answers to the practice tests are contained in a section at the end of the book.

CHAPTER 2

GETTING ACQUAINTED WITH YOUR IBM PERSONAL COMPUTER

Since your first contact with the computer may seem a bit strange and complicated, we will proceed very slowly. Rest assured that after a few sessions, routine operations will seem very natural and will cause you no trouble. Initially, though, be prepared for a certain "confusion quotient." Don't hesitate to review previously studied material, if needed.

2—1 OBJECTIVES

In this chapter we want to become familiar with the computer and start learning how it operates. No BASIC programming will be done until the next chapter. However, learning how the keyboard operates and how information is entered and modified is fundamental to all that will follow. This material is easy to master, but do make sure that you understand the objectives thoroughly as you progress.

Connecting The Computer To Your TV Display

The IBM Monochrome Display with the Monochrome Adapter can be used with this text except for Chapter 4 and a few examples involving graphics. For these, you will need the IBM Color/Graphics Monitor Adapter and a color (or black and white) monitor/television set. See your *Guide to Operations* for details about how to connect the computer to one of these displays.

Direct Mode

One of the easiest ways to use the computer is in the direct mode. No programming is involved; rather the computer carries out instructions as they are entered. In due time we will learn how to do much more. However, for the present, simple operations in the direct mode are a nice introduction to using the computer.

Screen Editing

Rarely is information entered into a computer without making mistakes. We need to be able to easily change or correct material that has been entered. A thorough knowledge of this capability will save you a great deal of time later on.

2—2 DISCOVERY ACTIVITIES

Before beginning work on the computer, we must establish several important points. On a typewriter, the L is often used for the numeral 1. A different key is used, however, on the computer. The numeral 1 is found with the other numeral keys along the top row of the keyboard. One of the most frequent mistakes made by the beginner is to type L when the numeral 1 is desired. Next, do not use the upper case or lower case letter O for the numeral 0. Like the numeral 1, the 0 is found along the top row of the keyboard. Although there are numerals on the keypad to the right of the keyboard, we will prefer to use the arrows and other functions on these keys. (See the *BASIC* reference manual for use of these keys as a numeric keypad.)

■ **Don't use the L for the 1!**
Don't use the Oh for the 0!

Now we are ready to begin work. Sit down in front of the computer, get comfortable, and let's go! Locate the key marked ↵ just above the **PrtSc** key on the keyboard. This ↵ key is the ENTER key, and will be referred to as the ENTER key most of the time. You will use it often. Also, locate the keys marked ⇧ on either side of the keyboard. These are the shift keys.

1. First, turn on the TV (if necessary). Place the IBM DOS diskette in drive A and close the door (see the *DOS* reference manual, Chapter 1). Now turn on the computer with the red switch at the rear of the right-hand side of the cabinet.

After about 30 seconds or so, you will see the message

```
Current date is Tue 1-01-1980
Enter new date: _
```

or something similar depending on your version of the DOS diskette. Refer to Chapter 2 in the *DOS* reference manual. Enter the date in the required format (for example, 11–5–82) and press ENTER (the key marked ←┘). Now you will see the message

```
Current time is 0:00:21.47
Enter new time: _
```

Enter the new time in the required format (for example, 9:07) and again press ENTER (←┘), or just press ENTER. On the screen you will see

```
The IBM Personal Computer DOS
Version 1.10 (C) Copyright IBM Corp 1981, 1982
A>_
```

Now type

BASICA (Capital letters or lower case letters may be used.)

and press ENTER (←┘). In a few moments, you will see

```
The IBM Personal Computer Basic
Version A1.10 Copyright IBM Corp.  1981, 1982
19323 Bytes free
Ok
_
```

(On your machine, the number of **Bytes free** and the **Version** number may differ.) If you do not see these messages, start the procedure over again. The blinking underscore is called a cursor. It will be displayed on the screen most of the time.

2. Type in the following.

```
WIDTH 40
```

Now press ENTER (the ← key) and watch your screen. Next type in

```
WIDTH 80
```

and watch your screen as you press ENTER ←. The WIDTH command can make things more readable on your screen.

3. Now type

```
PRINT 1+4
```

and stop. Has anything happened?

____

Now press ENTER and record below what happened.

____

4. Now you know how to make the computer do addition. Let's explore this some more. Type

```
PRINT 20.1+54
```

and press ENTER. What happened?

____

5. Type

```
PRINT 2+4-3
```

and press ENTER. Record the output below.

____

6. All right, the + and – are simple enough. Type the following expression

```
PRINT 12/2
```

and press ENTER. What happened?

got 6
___

What arithmetic operation does the / call for?

division
___

7. If, when typing in material, you make an error, you can move the cursor (blinking underscore) back to the error by pressing the key marked ← located just above the ENTER key. We will refer to the ← key as the backspace key. Each time the backspace key is pressed, the cursor will move one place to the left, erasing a character. When you reach the error, retype the line correctly. When you press the ENTER key, the computer may come back with `Syntax error`. If this happens, try to see what the problem is and retype the line.

8. Your TV screen should be fairly full now. Type CLS and press the ENTER key. What happened?

got clear skreen
___

Typing CLS and pressing the ENTER key clears the screen.

9. Now that you know how, you can clear the screen any time you desire. If the screen is full and new lines are entered, old lines will scroll off the top. Let's go on exploring the direct mode. Type

```
PRINT 2*50
```

and press ENTER. What happened?

got 100
___

What arithmetic operation is called for by the *?

____

10. Type in the following expression but don't press the ENTER key when finished.

```
PRINT (2+3)*4-1
```

What do you think will happen when you press ENTER?

____

Press ENTER and record below what did happen.

____

11. Now on to a new wrinkle. Type

```
PRINT "(2+3)*4-1"
```

And press ENTER. What did the computer do?

____

12. What will happen if you type

```
PRINT "BAD DOG"
```

And press ENTER?

____

Try it and see if you were correct.

13. Now let's move on to a different topic. First, clear the screen. If you have forgotten how, look back at Step 6. Type the following line. Press the ENTER key when through.

```
GRADE = 95
```

Now type

```
PRINT GRADE
```

And press ENTER. What happened?

____

4. Let's go on with this new idea. Take a few moments to examine the lines below.

```
LENGTH = 10
DEPTH = 6
HEIGHT = 4
VOLUME = LENGTH*DEPTH*HEIGHT
PRINT VOLUME
```

What do you think the computer will do if you type in these lines?

____

Now type in the lines remembering to press ENTER at the end of each line. What happened?

____

5. Study the lines below briefly.

```
LENGTH = 12
DEPTH = 9
SQYDS = (LENGTH*DEPTH)/9
PRINT SQYDS,"SQYDS"
```

What will the computer do with these instructions?

____

Clear the screen and type in the lines. Remember to press ENTER after each line. What did the computer do?

____

16. All right, let's go on to a different topic. Clear the screen and type the following lines. Remember to put in spaces where indicated. At the end of each line press the ENTER key. Make sure the volume control on the TV display is up.

```
SOUND 253,20
SOUND 340,40
```

You should have heard some pure tones on the computer. Did you?

____

Experiment with this a bit more. In particular, try setting the duration (second number) to 5 and 100. Try other values for the frequency (first number). Stay in the range of 37 to 32757 for the frequency. After a few trials, you should be able to figure out how the SOUND statement works.

17. This concludes the discovery material for now. Turn off the IBM Personal Computer and the TV display (if necessary).

2–3 DISCUSSION

Now we will go back over the topics that you have just worked with on the computer. With this experience, you will be in a far better position to understand the discussion.

Turning The Computer On and Off

The computer is simplicity itself to turn ON and OFF! As you have already seen, this is done with the switch at the right rear of the computer cabinet. However, in order to bring up BASICA (Advanced BASIC), you must first place the IBM DOS diskette in drive A before turning the computer on. Then, after typing in the date and pressing ENTER and typing in the time and pressing ENTER, you will get a message that has a last line that looks like

```
A>_
```

At this point, you type BASICA and press ENTER. You will then bring up BASICA and you will know you are in the Advanced BASIC mode when the last line on the screen reads

```
Ok
_
```

One important point; if at any time things get away from you, if you have lost touch, or if the computer seems out of control, you have a foolproof escape mechanism. Simply hold down the **Ctrl** key and the **Alt** key, while pressing the **Del** key. This puts you back at the initial level encountered when the computer is turned on. This remedy is not without disadvantage, however, since you will lose any programs or information in memory when you recover in this manner.

Direct Mode

In the discovery activities, you learned how to do simple arithmetic operations using the computer like a simple calculator. This is also known as the direct mode. As we shall see in the next chapter, BASIC stores instructions and commands in a series of numbered lines, and then is directed by you to perform all the instructions at the same time. If, however, the instructions are typed in without a line number, the computer assumes you want a direct or immediate answer and does what you asked it to do, if possible.

When material is typed in, nothing happens until you press ENTER. The ENTER key tells the computer you are through typing the information. Remember, when you are through typing anything at all and want to let the computer know, press the ENTER key.

There are a few cases where the computer responds to a single keystroke and does not require that the ENTER key be pressed. However, such cases are the exception rather than the rule.

We have discovered that addition and subtraction are called for by + and –, which probably wasn't much of a surprise! Multiplication and division are indicated by * and /, respectively. Parentheses can be used to group operations any way desired. There are a number of other clever operations that can be done, but we will postpone discussion of these to later chapters. If you type

```
PRINT 5*3.2+6.3
```

and press ENTER, the computer will carry out the arithmetic and print the result.

If you type

```
PRINT "ABCDEFG"
```

and press ENTER, the computer is instructed to print out the collection of characters between the quotation marks-in this case the letters ABCDEFG. Such a collection is called a "character string," and is an important concept which we will return to throughout the balance of the book.

The computer can keep track of a number of pieces of information in the direct mode. Thus

```
A = 2
B = 3
PRINT A+B
```

will cause 5 to be printed on the screen. There is a very important point in connection with this concept. If we type

```
PRINT TAX
```

and press ENTER, the numeral zero will be displayed. Since we gave no value to TAX, the computer assigned the value 0 and then printed it out.

The computer is very relaxed about names for quantities used either in the direct mode or in BASIC programs. We can use "long" names like DEPTH or RATE as well as "short" names like D or R. However, this ability to use long names does create something to be careful about. These long names must be typed correctly each time they are used. Also, spaces are not allowed in names. Certain words cannot be used for variable names since they are reserved for use by the computer. See the *BASIC* reference manual for a list of "reserved words."

This very brief introduction to the notion of variable names suffices for our discussion of the direct mode. We will return for a more complete discussion of the concept later in the book.

Screen Editing

The IBM Personal Computer has line editing commands that can be used to make changes. These are most effective when used to modify BASIC programs. However, since some of the commands can be used in the direct mode, we should look at the process in detail. We will limit our discussion to changes in a line before the ENTER key has been pressed. First, the cursor can be moved to the left with the backspace key. As mentioned earlier, the backspace key erases a character to the left of the cursor each time it is pressed. The correction can be made and typing can resume from that point. In addition, the cursor can be moved back and forth with the left arrow and right arrow keys found on the lower right-hand side of the keyboard. The important feature of these keys is that the cursor can be moved over characters without changing them. If a character is typed, that character replaces the character above the cursor.

We can also insert or delete characters in a line. If you press the **Ins** key and then type characters, the new material is inserted in the line beginning at the position of the cursor. The old material is shifted to the right as the new characters are inserted. In order to turn off the insert mode, you simply press the **Ins** key again. If the **Del** key is pressed, the character above the cursor is deleted and all material to the right is shifted left one place. By pressing the **Del** key several times, as many characters as desired can be deleted from a line. It is not necessary to "turn off" the delete mode as was necessary with the insert mode.

These simple editing commands can be used in the direct mode to make changes or corrections. In the next chapter, we will see much more powerful editing commands.

2–4 PRACTICE TEST

Take the test below to discover how well you have learned the objectives of Chapter 2. The answers to the practice test are given at the end of the book.

1. When you are through typing a line, how do you let the computer know?

____

2. If you lose control of the computer, how can you regain it?

____

3. What symbol is used to indicate multiplication on the computer?

4. How do you clear the screen display?

5. What operation does the symbol / indicate?

6. What will happen if you type

```
PRINT 3*4/6
```

and then press ENTER?

7. What will happen if you type

```
PRINT "25/5+2"
```

and then press ENTER?

8. Suppose you type PRING 2+3*4 and before you press ENTER, you notice a G is where a T should be in the word PRINT. Describe a way to correct this.

CHAPTER 3

INTRODUCTION TO BASIC

Now we are ready to begin learning about programming in BASIC. In this chapter we will see how to write and execute some very simple programs.

3—1 OBJECTIVES

The objectives of this chapter are simple but important as they are your first introduction to BASIC. The objectives are listed below.

Requirements for BASIC Programs

All BASIC programs have common characteristics. We will look at some very simple programs to learn about these characteristics.

Telling the Computer What to Do

Commands are used to tell the computer to do something to or with a BASIC program. These action words are used to control a program. We will look at the following commands: LIST, RUN, NEW, RENUM, and AUTO.

Entering and Controlling Programs

This objective overlaps the one above. The main thing we want to accomplish is to make you comfortable while entering and controlling programs. All the programs we will encounter initially are short and easy to handle.

Variable Names in BASIC

We must know how to name either numbers or strings of characters in BASIC programs. Fortunately, the computer has very relaxed rules about this.

3–2 DISCOVERY EXERCISES

In the discovery activities that follow, you will be directed to enter various programs. If you see an ⟨ENTER⟩ in the instructions, press the ENTER (↵) key. Remember from your experiences in Chapter 2 that pressing the ENTER key tells the computer you are through typing. Now go on to the activities below.

Computer Work

1. Turn on your computer and bring up BASICA.

2. Type in

```
100 LET A=1 <ENTER>
```

This is the first line of a BASIC program.

3. Now type in the balance of the program as listed below.

```
110 LET B=8 <ENTER>
120 LET C=A+B <ENTER>
130 PRINT C <ENTER>
140 END <ENTER>
```

If you make mistakes while typing in the program, either retype the line or correct it using the methods learned in Chapter 2.

4. Clear the screen using the CLS command. What happened to the program you just typed in?

5. Fortunately, all is not lost. The computer has remembered what you typed in even though the screen is blank. Type LIST and press the ENTER key. What happened?

6. On the TV display you should see the program just entered. For the time being ignore the line numbers at the beginning of each line. Just read the lines in the program and try to get a sense of what they mean. If the computer is told to carry out the instructions, what do you think will happen?

____

Type RUN and press the ENTER key. What did happen?

____

7. All right, now type

```
110 LET B=5 <ENTER>
```

Clear the screen, type LIST, and then press the ENTER key. What has happened to line 110 in the program?

____

8. If you tell the computer to execute this program what do you think will happen?

____

Type RUN , press the ENTER key, and record what happened. Were you right?

____

9. Now type

```
140 <ENTER>
```

clear the screen and display the program using the LIST command. What has happened to line 140?

____

If you want to delete a line in a BASIC program, how do you do it?

____

10. Now RUN the program. What happened?

____

Does the END statement that formerly was in line 140 appear to be required by the computer?

____

11. Let's experiment a bit more. Often we want to clear out the program in the computer's memory. This is done with the NEW command. Type NEW and press the ENTER key. What happened?

____

Type LIST and press the ENTER key to see what the computer has in memory. Is anything there?

____

12. We have learned how to clear out a program in memory, but now have no program left! To get our program back we must enter it again. Type in the program below.

```
100 LET A=1 <ENTER>
110 LET B=8 <ENTER>
120 LET C=A+B <ENTER>
130 PRINT C <ENTER>
140 END <ENTER>
```

check all the lines to make sure they were entered correctly. If a line needs to be changed, retype it. If you had to retype lines, clear the screen with the CLS command and redisplay the program by typing LIST.

3. Now type

```
125 LET D=B-A <ENTER>
135 PRINT D <ENTER>
```

Clear the screen and display the program. What has happened?

4. Take a few moments to study the program. What will happen if you RUN the program?

Type RUN, press the ENTER key, and record below what the computer did.

5. In the original program the line numbers were not consecutive (line 100, 101, 102, 103, etc.) but had gaps (e.g., 100, 110, 120, 130, and 140). Can you think of a reason for doing this now? (Hint: See step 13.)

6. How do you insert lines in a BASIC program? (Hint: See Steps 13 and 15.)

7. Clear out the program in memory by typing NEW and pressing the ENTER key. Enter the program below.

```
100 INPUT WHITE <ENTER>
110 LET RED=WHITE+2 <ENTER>
120 PRINT RED <ENTER>
130 GOTO 100 <ENTER>
140 END <ENTER>
```

18. This new program has several features that you have not seen before. Study the program carefully and think about what will happen if we RUN the program. What does the GOTO 100 in line 130 mean?

______

19. RUN the program and record what the computer did.

______

Type the numeral 6 and press the ENTER key. What happened?

______

20. Type the numeral 10 and press the ENTER key. What took place?

______

21. What line in the program do you think is generating the question mark?

______

Describe in your own words what the program is doing. If necessary, experiment some more to make sure you are correct.

______

22. Now we want to get out of the program. Press, and hold down, the **Ctrl** key (located at the left-hand side of the keyboard) and then press the **Break** key (found on the front side of the key marked **Scroll Lock** at the right uppermost part of the keyboard). From now on we will refer to this as "Ctrl-Break". What happened?

______

23. Clear out the program in memory. Type AUTO 100 and press ENTER. What happened?

______

After the 100 on the screen type

```
LET A=100 <ENTER>
```

Note that line number 110 is displayed for us. The AUTO command gives us line numbers automatically. Type in the rest of the program as follows

```
110 PRINT A <ENTER>
120 LET A=A+1 <ENTER>
130 GOTO 110 <ENTER>
140 END <ENTER>
```

To exit the AUTO mode, press Ctrl-Break. (See Step 22.)

4. RUN the program and record below what happened.

When you get tired of watching the display, press Ctrl-Break. What happened?

5. Try it once more. RUN the program and after a few numbers are typed out, interrupt the program. How do you stop a BASIC program running on the computer?

6. Clear the screen and display the program in memory. (See Step 5.) Type the lines below. Note the absence of spaces in the first line and the extra spaces in the second.

```
100LETA=1 <ENTER>
1 2 0 L E T A = A + 1 <ENTER>
```

Clear the screen and LIST the program. What happened?

Now type

```
125 PRINT A <ENTER>
```

and RUN the program. What happened?

____

Clearly, some spaces are important in BASIC statements. Just note the fact for now. We will return to this matter later. Press the ENTER key.

27. Let's try a program with some new features. Clear the program from memory by typing NEW and then pressing the ENTER key. Type in the program below. For automatic line numbering, type AUTO 100.

```
100 PRINT "TYPE A NUMBER" <ENTER>
110 INPUT FIRST <ENTER>
120 PRINT "ONE MORE TIME" <ENTER>
130 INPUT SECOND <ENTER>
140 LET SUM=FIRST + SECOND <ENTER>
150 PRINT "THEIR SUM IS" <ENTER>
160 PRINT SUM <ENTER>
170 END <ENTER>
```

28. Study the program for a few moments. Now RUN the program. What happened?

____

Type the numeral 12, press the ENTER key, and record below what the computer did.

____

29. All right, now type the numeral 13, press the ENTER key, and record below what happened.

____

30. Now type in

```
EDIT 120 <ENTER>
```

Move the cursor to the T in TIME using the right arrow under the 6 on the far right of the keyboard. Replace TIME" with NUMBER PLEASE" and press ENTER. Run the program again.

31. This simple program illustrates that we can arrange for BASIC programs to print out curt or courteous messages as well as numbers.

32. Now let's look at a different topic. Clear the screen. Type NEW and press the ENTER key to clear the program from memory. Then enter the following program. Before you do, press and hold down the key marked Alt (at the lower left-hand corner of the keyboard) and press the A key. Type 100 and press ENTER. Now proceed to enter the program.

```
100 LET A=1 <ENTER>
110 LET A$ ="HOUSE" <ENTER>
120 PRINT A <ENTER>
130 PRINT "A" <ENTER>
140 PRINT A$<ENTER>
150 PRINT "A$" <ENTER>
160 END <ENTER>
```

33. This program contains something new. Look at the A$ in line 110. Note that it is set equal to a word enclosed in quotation marks. The balance of the program has to do with variations on printing out A and A$. RUN the program and record the output.

____

34. Study the output carefully and identify what was printed in response to each of the PRINT statements. For the time being just make the comparison. Later we will examine the subject in detail. Enter the following line:

```
155 PRINT B <ENTER>
```

35. Clear the screen and display the program with the LIST command. Note that the only place B is mentioned is in line 155 in the PRINT statement. What do you think will happen if we RUN the program?

____

All right, now RUN the program and record what happened.

____

36. As you saw in Chapter 2, even though the value of B was not defined in the program, the computer assigned it a value of 0. This is an important fact to be remembered while writing programs.

37. Now we want to look at something that can help you a great deal while writing programs. Clear the screen and display the program. Focus your attention on the line numbers. Now type RENUM 1000,,10. (Note the two commas.) and press the ENTER key. Display the program. What has happened?

____

38. Let's try this once more. Type RENUM 200,,5 and press the ENTER key. Display the program. Now what happened?

____

39. One last time. Type RENUM and press the ENTER key. Display the program and record what happened.

____

Do you see the purpose of the RENUM command?

____

40. This concludes the discovery activities for this chapter. Turn off the computer and go on to the next section.

3—3 DISCUSSION

Now that you have been through the discovery activities on your computer and have seen some of the features of BASIC in action, we can summarize what has taken place.

Correcting Mistakes

Since most of us make mistakes while typing, we need to be able to correct errors. Suppose a mistake is made while you are typing a line. How it is corrected depends upon whether you have pressed the ENTER key yet. If you are on the line containing the error, you can move the cursor left using the left arrow key, right using the right arrow key, and make corrections as you saw in Chapter 2. Also, if necessary, you can insert or delete characters using the **Ins** and **Del** keys. When all the corrections are made in a line, press the ENTER key. Note that the cursor does not have to be at the right end of the line when ENTER is pressed.

If you wish to change a line after pressing the ENTER key, then you may use the EDIT command. For example, if you wish to change line 110 in a program, you should type in

```
EDIT 110 <ENTER>
```

The computer will display line 110 with the cursor on that line. You may now correct the line as discussed above.

If the computer detects a syntax error while the program is being RUN, it will type out an error message and the number of the line in which the error occurs. In addition, the line will be displayed on the screen with the cursor on that line. The line may now be corrected as discussed above.

Remember to press the ENTER key when all corrections on a line are completed. For more advanced full-screen editing features, consult the *BASIC* reference manual.

Requirements For BASIC Programs

Several important facts about BASIC programs have been demonstrated. To have a program to use for discussion purposes, we will return to the original program used in the computer work:

```
100 LET A=1
110 LET B=8
120 LET C=A+B
130 PRINT C
140 END
```

Each BASIC program consists of a group of lines called statements. Each statement must have a line number. In the program above, there are three types of BASIC statements: LET, PRINT, and END. The first two statements will be treated fully in the next chapter. For the time being the use of each of these statements in the program is clear. The END statement is not required with the IBM Personal Computer. The program will execute with or without the END statement. However, it is a good practice to use it, especially in long programs, so there will be no confusion with regard to where the program ends. We will make it a rule to use the END statement in all programs even though the computer doesn't require it.

Generally the line numbers in a BASIC program are not numbered consecutively (such as 100, 101, 102, etc.). The reason is that we may want to insert additional statements later if we discover errors or want to modify the program. If the lines were numbered consecutively spaced 1 apart, it would be less convenient to make changes. With gaps in the line numbers, statements can be inserted by simply typing in the new statements using line numbers not already in the program.

The automatic line numbering feature is one you may want to use often. In the Discovery Exercises, we typed AUTO 100 to automatically produce the line numbers 100, 110, 120, etc. By typing AUTO I,J ⟨ENTER⟩, the computer will automatically produce line numbers starting with I and increasing in steps of J. Thus, AUTO 100,50 will produce lines numbered 100, 150, 200, 250, etc. If the value of J is omitted, the step size will be 10, as you have seen in the Discovery Exercises. If the values of both I and J are omitted, then the first line will be 10 and the step size will also be 10. So AUTO ⟨ENTER⟩ will produce lines numbered 10, 20, 30, etc. We exit the AUTO mode by pressing Ctrl-Break. You can also obtain AUTO by pressing, and holding down, the Alt key and pressing the A key. The Alt key has numerous other similar uses. (See Chapter 2 of your *BASIC* reference manual.)

Quite often we want to sort out the line numbers in a program after changes have been made. This has nothing to do with the execution of the program, but merely makes the program look nicer or allows more line insertions, if needed. The renumber command is used to renumber the lines in a program. RENUM 1000,540,100 would leave all of the line numbers up to 540 of the program in memory as they were and renumber line 540 as 1000 with each line thereafter renumbered as 1100, 1200, etc. By typing RENUM I,J,K where I, J, and K are whole numbers, the program lines are renumbered using I as the first number, starting at J in the program in memory, and spaced K apart.

If you wish to, you can renumber all of the lines of a program, by omitting the value of J as we saw in the Discovery Exercises. Thus, RENUM 500,,20 would number the first line in the program 500. The second line would be 520, the third 540, and so on.

Later on we will discover that BASIC programs can branch to any line numbers in the program. The renumber command takes care of these branch line numbers as well as the lines themselves.

As we saw in the Discovery Exercises, some spaces are important in BASIC programs. It would be time ill used to discuss this topic at any length. It is, however, good to keep spaces in the back of your mind as a possible solution to errors that come up. Suffice it to say that if you make your program statements readable, you should have no problems with spaces.

BASIC does not care in what order the lines are entered. If, for example, we type

```
140 END
120 LET C=A+B
110 LET B=8
130 PRINT C
100 LET A=1
```

and this new program is displayed, the computer will sort out the statements and display them in numerical order. In the same way, if we were to execute the program as typed above, the computer would first sort the statements into the proper order before starting execution.

You can remove a BASIC statement from the program by typing the line number and pressing the ENTER key. Statements can be modified by retyping the lines involved, pressing the ENTER key after each line is typed, or by using the EDIT command. As indicated above, statements can be added by using line numbers not already in the program. Thus, BASIC statements can be added, removed, or changed as desired. This ability to change programs easily is one of the powerful characteristics of BASIC on the IBM Personal Computer.

Telling the Computer What To Do

We must make a sharp distinction between the statements in a BASIC program and commands. Commands tell the computer to do something with a program. We have seen several of these in the computer work and will briefly review the use of each.

When a BASIC program is entered, it goes into memory. Quite often you need to see the program contained in memory. This could be because of changes made in the program, or perhaps you simply need a copy of the program. In any case, you already know this is done with the LIST command. The wise programmer will make valuable use of this command. If a program doesn't work as it should, your first step should be to display the program in memory. Often you and the computer may be in a state of mutual confusion about the program in memory. The way to resolve the issue is to have the computer furnish a copy of the program that it is executing. Use this copy to troubleshoot the program.

When you turn off the computer, the contents of memory are cleared out automatically. While working on the computer, however, it is possible to get programs mixed together. Suppose you are working with one program and decide to go on to another. If you don't clear the first program out of memory, the second program will go in right over the first with the result that parts of both programs may be in memory. The way to avoid doing this is to be careful to clear out (or erase) a program with the NEW command when you are through with it.

A BASIC program is simply a set of instructions to be acted upon by the computer. However, the computer needs to be told to start this process. When the RUN command is received, the computer goes to the lowest numbered statement in the program, carries out the instructions, goes to the next higher numbered statement, and keeps on carrying out instructions in numerical order, unless the program directs a statement to be done out of order.

Entering and Controlling Programs

So far, when you have been instructed to type in programs or commands, the ⟨ENTER⟩ prompt was given to remind you to press the ENTER key. This habit should be well developed now, so we will not use the ⟨ENTER⟩ prompt in the future. From now on, when you are through typing a statement or command, press the ENTER key to let the computer know you are finished.

Situations come up where we need to be able to control a program that is running. Certainly one of the most dramatic cases is when a program is in a closed loop and will keep on running forever if we don't interrupt it. We can break into such a program by holding down the Ctrl key and pressing the Break key (Ctrl-Break). When this is done, the computer breaks the program execution, tells us Break in (whatever line was being processed when the interruption took place). A different situation occurs when the computer is in an input loop waiting for a number to be typed in. If we want to get out of such a situation, we again press Ctrl-Break. The computer then jumps out of the program execution back to the **Ok** mode.

Variable Names in BASIC

Now we come to one of the ideas in BASIC that most often causes problems for the beginner. It concerns variable names and the distinction between the name of the variable and the data stored under that name. In the BASIC statement

```
100 LET A = 2
```

the **A** names a variable. By "variable" we mean that different values can be assigned to **A**. Consequently, LET statements are often called assignment statements. In this case the variable **A** is assigned the value 2. Actually, what is taking place is that somewhere in the computer there is a memory location named **A**, and the number 2 is stored in that location. The fundamental idea is to separate the name of a location in memory from the contents of the memory locations. It's the same notion as the difference between a post office box number and the contents of that box. The box number does not change, but the contents of the box may be changed at any time.

The use of LET in the assignment statement is optional. As far as the computer is concerned, you can use LET or not. In this book, we will always use LET in assignment statements for consistency's sake.

Consider the following statement.

```
130 LET C=A+B
```

This instructs the computer to get the numbers stored in locations named A and B, add them together, and put the sum in the storage location named C. The equal sign means to evaluate what is on the right and assign it to the variable name on the left. To pursue this issue further, suppose we have a BASIC statement such as

```
120 LET B = B+1
```

If we consider the statement above as an algebraic equation, we have

$$B = B + 1$$

If we subtract B from both sides of this equation, we have

$$0 = 1$$

which is very strange indeed! It is certainly clear that in a BASIC statement, the = sign does not mean the same as it does in an algebraic equation. Instead, the statement

```
120 LET B = B+1
```

instructs the computer to get the number stored in location **B**, add 1 to the number, and put the result back in the storage location named **B**.

If we store a number in a location, anything that was stored there before is lost. Consider the following statements:

```
100 LET A = 1
110 LET A = 2*3
```

Line 100 instructs the computer to set up a location called **A** and put the number 1 in that location. Line 110 tells the computer to multiply 2 by 3 and store the product in location **A**. The 1 stored previously in location **A** has been lost.

This brings us to the heart of the issue. The letter **A**, which identifies a location, is called a variable because the contents of **A** can be changed. The name of the location does not change, but the number stored there can be.

To be precise, the variable **A** referred to above is called a "numeric" variable. The reason for including "numeric" in the name is that there is another type of variable called a "character string." You were introduced to this concept briefly in the discovery activities, and now we must tie up some loose ends.

As far as names are concerned, it is easy to distinguish between numeric and character-string variables. A, BOOK, M, and P would all identify numeric variables and name numeric quantities. A$,

BOOK$, M$, and P$ all name strings of characters. The $ symbol that is appended identifies the name as a character-string variable. In the BASIC statement

```
100 LET B$="BARN"
```

B$ names a location in memory in which the character string "BARN" is stored. The quotation marks set off the string, but are not part of it.

Recall that the IBM Personal Computer has very relaxed rules for variable names. It allows you to use "long" names for numeric variables as well as character strings. You can use up to 40 characters (including the $ character in the case of character strings) in long names. The computer has a set of "reserved" words that are used in BASIC and for commands. These words cannot be used to name variables. See the *BASIC* reference manual for the list of reserved words. If you make a mistake and use one, however, the computer will let you know!

Let's go over the important points once more. A variable name in BASIC identifies a storage location in memory that can contain a number or character string. The contents of the storage location (the value of the variable) may be changed, but the name of the location cannot.

The LET (or assignment) statement evaluates what is on the right side of the equal sign and assigns it to the storage location named on the left side. Thus,

```
100 LET D = A+B+C
```

instructs the computer to evaluate the expression (A+B+C) using the numbers stored in memory locations named A, B, and C. The result is then stored in the memory location named D.

We have just scratched the surface with regard to character-string variables. We will return to this topic several times during the balance of the book.

3—4 PRACTICE TEST

Take the test below to discover how well you have learned the objectives of Chapter 3. The answers to the practice test are given at the end of the book.

1. How do you signal the computer that you are through typing a line or instruction?

2. Suppose that your computer is waiting at an INPUT statement in a program for you to enter a number. You decide instead that you want to jump the computer out of the program. How do you do this?

3. How do you interrupt a program that is running on your computer?

4. What is wrong with the following program?

```
100 LET A=1
110 LET B=3
120 LET C=B-A
PRINT C
130 END
```

5. What will happen if the program in question 4 were corrected and RUN?

6. How long can "long" variable names be?

7. How do you insert a line in a BASIC program?

8. How do you replace a line in a BASIC program?

____

9. How do you remove a line from a BASIC program?

____

10. How do you display the program in memory?

____

11. How do you erase the screen?

____

12. How do you command the computer to execute the program in memory?

____

13. How do you erase a program in memory?

____

14. What is the difference between a numeric and a character-string variable?

____

15. What will the following EDIT command do?

```
EDIT 120
```

____

CHAPTER 4

GRAPHICS AND SOUND

4—1 OBJECTIVES

In this chapter we will discuss the graphics and music sub-language statements that are available in BASICA for the IBM Personal Computer. For the graphics exercises you will need the Color/Graphics Display Adapter and a monitor/television set.

Drawing lines

Straight lines are the basic component of many kinds of shapes and figures. Drawing lines easily and quickly is a necessary first step in learning to make complex drawings on the display screen.

Drawing and Naming Shapes

The ability to draw and name shapes allows for additional flexibility in making shapes and figures with your computer.

Coloring in Shapes

Colors make shapes and figures more interesting and attractive. We must know how to color or shade in areas of the screen display. (A color monitor/television set is helpful but not necessary.)

Musical Notes

In order to make music, we must be able to generate notes. We will need to make notes of different lengths and in different octaves.

Music

Songs consist of musical phrases made up of notes. To create a song, we must learn to make and name musical phrases.

4—2 DISCOVERY EXERCISES

Computer Work

1. Turn on the computer and bring up BASICA. Type

```
SCREEN 1 <ENTER>
```

This statement places the computer in a graphics mode.

2. Type the following statements. Remember to press ENTER at the end of each line.

```
KEY 1,"DRAW " + CHR$(34)
KEY 5,"CLS" + CHR$(13)
```

At the bottom of the screen observe that DRAW " and CLS← now appear. CHR$(34) puts the quotation mark after DRAW and CHR$(13) puts the left arrow after CLS. DRAW " is now stored in the key marked F1 and CLS← is stored in the key marked F5.

Press the key marked F1 on the far left of the keyboard. What happened?

____

Press ⟨ENTER⟩ and then press F5. What happened?

____

The KEY statements given in direct mode have made function key F1 print out DRAW " and function key F5 print out CLS⟨ENTER⟩. Pressing F5 executes the CLS statement while pressing F1 displays DRAW " on the screen.

3. Using function key F1 type

```
DRAW "L60" <ENTER>
```

What happened?

____

If "illegal function call" appears on the screen, then you should refer to Appendix A.

4. Using function key F1, type

```
DRAW "U60"
DRAW "R60"
DRAW "D60"
```

What figure now appears on the screen?

___

What words can you match up with L,R,U,D?

___

5. Clear the sreen by pressing F5 and type in the following lines. Be sure to watch the screen as you press ENTER.

```
DRAW "E60"
DRAW "F60"
DRAW "G60"
DRAW "H60"
```

Complete the following diagram of the substatements that draw the diamond.

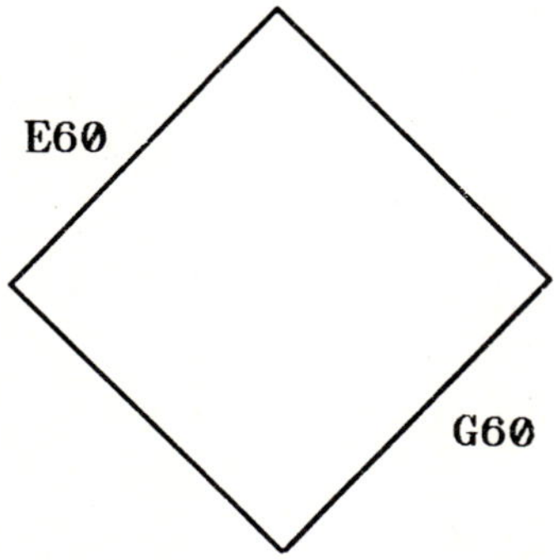

6. Type the following line. Watch the screen as you press ENTER.

```
DRAW "R60 U60 L60 D60"
```

Draw the combination of figures that appear on the screen.

Are the squares the same size?

Where does drawing begin with the DRAW statement?

7. Clear the screen using F5 and type the following statements.

```
DRAW "NE60"
DRAW "NF60"
DRAW "NG60"
DRAW "NH60"
```

What does N do? (See Step 5.)

. Clear the memory with the NEW command. Clear the screen and type the following program.

```
100 CLS
200 LET BOX$ = "R40 U20 L40 D20"
300 DRAW BOX$
400 END
```

(Notice that there are no quotation marks around BOX$.) Run the program. Draw the box that appears on the screen. Be sure to get the relative proportions correct.

. Edit line 200 using the EDIT command by inserting a B as follows.

```
200 LET BOX$ = "R40 BU20 L40 D20"
```

Run the program. What has changed in the figure?

What does the B do?

. Edit line 200 by inserting another B as follows.

```
200 LET BOX$ = "R40 BU20 BL40 D20"
```

What kind of figure will be drawn when you run this program?

Run the program. Were you correct?

11. Clear the screen and list the program in memory. Edit out the B's in line 200 and add lines 310 and 320 so that the program looks like this when listed.

```
100 CLS
200 LET BOX$ = "R40 U20 L40 D20"
300 DRAW BOX$
310 LET DIAGONAL$ = "E40"
320 DRAW DIAGONAL$
400 END
```

Run the program. Does DRAW DIAGONAL$ draw a diagonal of the box?

____

12. Edit line 310 as follows.

```
310 LET DIAGONAL$ = "E20"
```

List the program. What do you think will happen when the program in memory is run?

____

Run the program. Were you right?

____

13. Edit line 310 as follows.

```
310 LET DIAGONAL$ = "NE20 F60"
```

Run the program. Draw a diagram of the figure on the screen. Try not to lift your pencil off the paper.

____

Where your pencil ends up is the place where the screen pen is now located on the figure. Now type (without a line number)

```
DRAW "L40"
```

Does the new line agree with where your pencil ended up?

Add line 250 as follows.

```
250 DRAW "S8"
```

Run the program. What happened?

Delete line 310, add line 240 and edit line 250 as follows.

```
240 INPUT SCALE
250 DRAW "S=SCALE;"
340 GOTO 240
```

Run the program. Input 2, 4, 8 and 14 when the question mark appears. Which scale number draws the same size rectangle as "R40 U20 L40 D20"?

4. Press Ctrl-Break to jump the program out of the loop. Clear the screen and add line 310 as follows.

```
310 LET DIAGONAL$ = "NE20 F60 L40 H20"
```

If this program is run and 4 is entered at the input prompt, what additions will be made to the following diagram.

Run the program. Input 4 as the scale number. Were you right?

____

You may wish to use these drawing statements to make some sketches of your own choosing.

15. Clear out the program in memory. Clear the screen and type in the following program.

```
10 INPUT A$
20 DRAW "X A$;"
30 GOTO 10
40 END
```

Run the program. Input the following string of characters at the question mark.

```
L40
D40
R40
U40
```

Where does each line start?

____

16. Press Ctrl-Break to jump the program out of the loop. Clear the screen and run the program again. Input 3 at the question mark. What happened?

____

17. Edit line 20 as follows.

```
20 DRAW "X A$; L50"
```

Run the program. Input the following strings of characters at the question mark.

```
E40
G40
D40 F40
```

What does L50 do in the program?

8. Jump the program out of the loop. Clear out the program in memory. Use F5 to clear the screen and type

```
PSET (160,100)
```

Look very carefully at the center of the screen. You will see a single point. PSET has set this point on the screen. Now type

```
PSET (319,0)
```

Before you hit ENTER, where will a point be set?

Press ENTER. Were you correct?

9. Clear the screen and then use F1 to type

```
DRAW "M319,199"
```

What does M319,199 do?

Clear the screen and then type

```
DRAW "M319,199H100"
```

What happened?

The numbers 319,199 locate the lower right-hand corner of the graphics screen. On some television sets this location will be off the screen.

Press F5 and type (using the F1 key)

```
DRAW "BM0,150R100"
```

At what point does the line begin?

___

The screen in this mode (medium resolution graphics) is 320 (from 0 to 319) points wide and 200 (from 0 to 199) points deep. The upper left hand corner is designated 0,0 and the lower right hand corner is designated 319,199 . The center of the screen is 160,100. The PSET statement requires parentheses around the numbers; the M substatement does not.

20. Let us look at two other graphics statements. Clear the screen. For convenience, we might set two more function keys as follows.

```
KEY 3,"CIRCLE ("
KEY 4,"PAINT ("
```

Notice that the parenthesis does not appear at the bottom of the screen.

Using function key F3, type

```
CIRCLE (240,120),30
```

Where is the center of the circle?

___

What is the radius of the circle?

___

Check your answers by typing

```
PSET (240,120)
DRAW "L30"
```

. Clear the screen and draw a circle and its center by typing

```
CIRCLE (240,120),30
PSET (240,120)
```

Now type

```
PAINT (240,120)
```

Did anything happen?

____

PAINT fills in a region out to its boundary. Because there is already a point set at 240,120, PAINT views the point as the boundary and does not fill in the circle.

Type

```
PAINT (240,119)
```

What happened?

____

Without using F4, type in the following (without parentheses).

```
PAINT 240,0
```

What happened?

____

The parentheses are required in the PAINT statement.
Type

```
PAINT (240,0)
```

What happened?

____

22. If you do not have a color monitor/television set go to Step 25. Clear the screen and type

```
SCREEN 0
DRAW "R50"
```

What happened?

____

The SCREEN 0 statement places the computer in text mode where graphics statements like DRAW are "illegal."
Type

```
SCREEN 1,0
```

The SCREEN 1,0 statement places the screen back in graphics mode again and allows colors other than black and white to appear.
Type

```
COLOR 4
```

What happened?

____

Your may need to adjust your color monitor/television set dials so that the background is red and the letters are white.
Type

```
COLOR 2
COLOR 1
```

What are the colors corresponding to 4, 2, and 1?

____

3. Clear the screen with F5 and type

```
COLOR 4,1
CIRCLE (240,120),40,3
```

What happened?

____

Type

```
PAINT (240,120),3,3
```

What happened?

____

Type

```
COLOR 1,1
```

What colors are the background and the interior of the circle (or ball) now?

____

Type

```
COLOR 3,1
```

What colors are the background and the ball now?

____

Type

```
COLOR 3,0
```

What colors are the background and the ball now?

____

Type

```
COLOR 0,1
```

What color is the background now?

____

Clear the memory and the screen.

24. We will examine the coloring capabilities of the IBM Personal Computer with the program below. Use the AUTO 100,100 numbering command and the function keys F3 and F4 to help you type the following program.

```
100 CLS
200 COLOR 1
300 CIRCLE (100,150),20,3
400 CIRCLE (160,150),20,3
500 CIRCLE (210,150),20,3
600 PAINT (100,150),1,3
700 PAINT (160,150),2,3
800 PAINT (210,150),3,3
900 END
```

Type Ctrl-Break to end automatic numbering. Run the program. What colors are the balls at the bottom of the screen?

____

Type

```
COLOR 2
```

What happened?

____

Type

```
COLOR 4
```

What happened?

____

Type

```
COLOR 4,0
```

What happened?

____

Type

```
COLOR 4,1
COLOR 4,0
COLOR 4,1
```

What happened to the colors of the balls?

____

Run the program again. Type

```
PAINT (160,100)
```

What happened?

____

The statement SCREEN 1,0 allows us to use color with graphics. In this graphics mode the COLOR statement varies the background color and the colors available for DRAWing and PAINTing on the selected background color. There are fifteen background colors and two sets of three colors each for drawing and painting.

25. Let's look at some musical BASIC statements. Clear the screen and clear out the program in memory using the NEW command. Type the following program.

```
100 PLAY "ABCDEFG"
200 END
```

Run the program. Was each note played higher than the last?

____

26. Edit line 100 as follows.

```
100 PLAY "CDEFGAB"
```

Run the program. Was each note played higher than the last?

____

27. Retype line 100 as follows.

```
100 PLAY "C1 E2 C4 E2"
```

Once again the spaces are for clarity. Run the program. Did the first or the last note last the longest? You may wish to run the program again to check your answer.

____

Edit line 100 as follows.

```
100 PLAY "O5 C1 E2 C4 E2"
```

Run the program. What does O5 do?

____

Add line 10.

```
10 PLAY "T60"
```

Display the program. Run the program. What happened to the length of the notes?

____

8. Edit line 100 as follows.

```
100 PLAY "C1 E4 T60 G8 B2"
```

Run the program. What pairs of notes lasted the same length of time? You may wish to run the program several times before you answer this question.

____

9. Edit line 100 by changing T60 to T240 as follows.

```
100 PLAY "C1 E4 T240 G8 B2"
```

Run the program. What notes are shorter than they were before?

____

10. Clear the memory and the screen and type in the following program.

```
100 LET WHITEBLACK$ = "CC#DD#EF G-GG#A B-BC"
110 LET WHITE$ = "CDEFGABC"
120 PLAY WHITE$ + WHITEBLACK$
130 END
```

Run the program. What notes in WHITE$ are repeated in WHITEBLACK$?

____

11. Clear out the program in memory. Type in the following program.

```
10 INPUT NOTES$
20 PLAY "O3 X NOTES$; O2; X NOTES$;"
30 GOTO 10
40 END
```

Run the program and enter the following string of notes at the question mark.

```
CEGA
BAGFE
```

Which string gave the nicest tune?

---

32. Jump the program out of the loop. To observe the use of graphics and sound together clear out the program in memory and type in the following program. There are some additional statements in this program that we have not discussed. Run the program after typing it in.

```
100 CLS
200 SCREEN 1,0
300 SONG$ ="E4F4G3A2"
400 HEAD$ ="L10U20R20D20L10"
500 BODY$ ="NG20NF20D30NG20NF20"
600 MOVE$ ="BM+40,0"
700 COLOR 0
800 CIRCLE (200,120),40
900 DRAW "BM40,40"
1000 DRAW HEAD$ + BODY$
1100 PLAY "MF"+SONG$
1200 DRAW MOVE$ + HEAD$ + BODY$
1300 PLAY "MF"+SONG$
1400 DRAW MOVE$ + HEAD$ + BODY$
1500 PLAY "MB"+"T60"+SONG$
1600 PAINT (200,120),1,3
1700 PAINT (200,120),2,3
1800 PAINT (200,120),3,3
1900 PAINT (200,120),0,3
2000 PAINT (0,0),2,3
2100 END
```

33. Turn off the computer.

4–3 DISCUSSION

The KEY Statement

The KEY statement allows us to change the meaning of the function keys. These function keys can then be used to assist us in entering commands and statements.

The direct mode statement **KEY 3,"PAINT("** stores PAINT(in function key F3. After this direct mode statement is entered, pressing F3 will place **PAINT(** on the screen at the current cursor position. All ten function keys may be defined in this manner.

Screen Modes

There are three screen modes. BASICA begins in screen mode 0 or text mode. **SCREEN 1,0** places the computer in medium resolution graphics mode with 320 by 200 points and color. Screen mode 2 has 640 by 200 points but does not allow color.

The Graphics Sublanguage

The IBM Personal Computer BASICA has a built in graphics sublanguage which is accessed through the DRAW statement. The DRAW statement can be used in either the direct or indirect mode as we saw in the Discovery Exercises.

The graphics sublanguage consists of the following statements:

	Statement	Meaning
Horizontal and Vertical Statements	L	Left
	R	Right
	U	Up
	D	Down
Diagonal Statements	E	Up and to the right
	F	Down and to the right
	G	Down and to the left
	H	Up and to the right
Move Statement	M number1,number2	Move to the location designated by number1,number2

These DRAW sublanguage graphics statements may be modified by letters before them and numbers after them. A letter "B" before a graphics statement moves the position of the graphics pen (or cursor) without drawing a line. A letter "N" before a statement executes the statement and then returns the cursor to the position it held before the statement was executed.

Numbers following the statement indicate how far the graphics cursor is to move horizontally, vertically or diagonally. The diagonal motion in the E,F,G,H statements is measured with respect to the horizontal direction. The length of the line drawn with diagonal sublanguage statements is always longer than the number of units used (about 1.4 times longer). For example,

```
DRAW "R20 U20 G20"
```

will draw a triangle.

The M (or move) statement moves the cursor to the location designated. If a plus or minus sign is used with either number1 or number2, then the meaning of the M statement changes. In this case, M moves the cursor horizontally number1 and vertically number2. Hence,

```
DRAW "BM0,0 M319,0 BM160,0 M160,199 M+0,30"
```

will draw a horizontal line across the top of the screen, a vertical line from the center to the bottom of the screen and then a short vertical line straight up.

The DRAW statement requires a string of characters and/or numbers. These characters or numbers can be stored in a string variable such as BOX$. If a string of substatements is given in a variable, such as BOX$, quotation marks are not required. If the substatements are given directly in the DRAW statement, then quotation marks are required around the string of substatements. For example, the program

```
100 CAP$ ="R20 U20 L40 D20 NR20 L20"
200 DRAW "ND90"+CAP$
300 END
```

will draw a pole with a cap on it.

Scale (S) and execute (X) are commands we have used to demonstrate the use of variables with sublanguage commands. The scale substatement determines the size of the objects to be drawn. If the scale is 4, the figure will be drawn the standard size. If the scale is 8, the figure will be drawn twice as large and if the scale is 2, the figure will be half as large.

The program

```
100 LET A = 8
200 DRAW "S=A; L10 D10 R10 U10"
300 END
```

will draw a box that is 20 on each side. The semicolon is required after each substatement that uses a variable.

The substatement X executes the string immediatley following it. For example, the program

```
100 LET FLAG$ = "E20 R20 G20 L20"
200 DRAW "ND90 X FLAG$;"
300 END
```

draws a flag on top of a pole. The semicolon is required after the X substatement.

We have not used the angle (A) substatement. Information concerning this draw substatement can be found in Chapter 4 of the *BASIC* reference manual.

Other BASICA Graphics Statements

In addition to the graphics sublanguage accessed by the graphics statement DRAW, we have used the graphics statements PSET, CIRCLE and PAINT. These statements all require a location enclosed in parentheses and may have color and boundary numbers as well. For example,

`PSET (240,150)`	Places a point at (240,150).
`CIRCLE (240,150),30`	Draws a circle of radius 30 in the lower right-hand corner of the screen.

There are four other graphics statements, PRESET, GET, PUT, and LINE, that we have not used. See the *BASIC* reference manual for further details.

Color

The SCREEN statement can be used to allow colors to appear on a color monitor/television set. The statement **SCREEN 1,0** allows colors to be displayed in the medium resolution graphics mode. The first number in a COLOR statement in graphics mode determines the color of the background (numbers 0 to 15). The number of each background color is given in the following table.

0	Black	8	Gray
1	Blue	9	Light Blue
2	Green	10	Light Green
3	Cyan	11	Light Cyan
4	Red	12	Light Red
5	Magenta	13	Light Magenta
6	Brown	14	Yellow
7	White	15	High Intensity White

The second number in a COLOR statement determines which of two groups of colors (0 or 1) will be used. The groups of colors or palettes consist of three colors each (numbered 1, 2, and 3). In palette 0,

1	is	Green
2	is	Red
3	is	Brown

In palette 1,

1	is	Cyan
2	is	Magenta
3	is	White

In both palettes, 0 is black.

The statement

```
COLOR 4,1
```

provides a red background and allows painting with palette 1. Lines can also be drawn in color.

Selection of a color for a circle or to fill in a region depends upon the palette fixed by the latest color statement.

`CIRCLE (160,100),60,2`	Draws a circle in palette color 2. If no number follows the radius, the circle will be drawn in palette color 3.
`PAINT (160,100),1,2`	Fills in a region with color 1 out to the boundary of color 2, where both colors are from the current palette.

Again, the actual color displayed depends upon the palette fixed by the latest COLOR statement.

For additional information on the interaction of the color and graphics statements, you should consult Chapter 3 and the COLOR statement in Chapter 4 of the *BASIC* reference manual.

The Music Sublanguage

The PLAY statement is similar to the DRAW statement in that it gives access to a musical sublanguage. C,D,E,F,G,A,B are the sublanguage statements that play notes. These statements can only be modified by a number, the symbol for flat (–), or a symbol for sharp (# or +) following the sublanguage statements.

A number after a note substatement determines the length of the note. The larger the number, the shorter the duration of the note. The note C4 will last twice as long as the note C8.

The octave of a note is determined by the 0 (octave) substatement. For example,

`PLAY "03C"`	will play middle C.
`PLAY "05C"`	will play high C.

Each one of the 7 octaves (0,1,2,3,4,5,6) starts at the C note.

The number of notes played per minute is determined by the T (tempo) substatement. A T60 substatement will set the computer to play 60 C4 notes per minute. T120, the starting tempo, will play 120 C4 notes per minute or 60 C2 notes per minute. The number following T must be between 32 and 255.

As with DRAW, PLAY requires a string of characters and numbers. The conventions about the use of quotation marks with explicit strings and string variables is the same as for the DRAW statement. There is a limit on the number of letters and numbers that can be contained between quotation marks in a PLAY statement. (See the *BASIC* reference manual.) It is, therefore, frequently necessary to put several strings of notes together to create longer compositions.

PLAY substatements, like DRAW substatements, can be used with variables.

The program

```
100 LET A = 5
110 PLAY "O = A; CDE"
120 END
```

will play CDE in octave 5 when executed.

The following PLAY statement will play the string of notes **NOTES$**.

```
PLAY "X NOTES$;"
```

Again, notice the semicolon at the end of the substatement before the " marks. This semicolon is required with the X (execute) substatement and with all substatements using variables.

The MF and MB substatements determine whether a string of notes will be played completely before the next BASIC statement is executed (Music Foreground) or while other BASIC statements are being executed (Music Background). This capability allows the computer to play musical tunes while it is drawing pictures.

There are some musical sublanguage statements we have not used. They can be found in Chapter 4 of the *BASIC* reference manual.

The following program will play part of a well-known song. Notice the use of P4 for a quarter note rest.

```
100 PLAY "E4E4E4F2F2G4F4E4D4E4F4G4C4F4E2D4C1"
200 PLAY "P4"
300 PLAY "E4E4E4F2F4G4F4E4D4E4F4G4C4F4E2D4C1"
```

4–4 PRACTICE TEST

Take the test below to discover how well you have learned the objectives of Chapter 4. The answers to the practice test are given at the end of the book.

1. What figure will the following direct mode statement draw when entered?

```
DRAW "BU20 L20 D40 R40 U40 L20"
```

2. What figure will the following direct mode statement draw when entered?

```
DRAW "E20 F20 L40 D40 R40 U40"
```

3. Write a direct mode statement that will draw the following diagram with the point (160,100) as indicated.

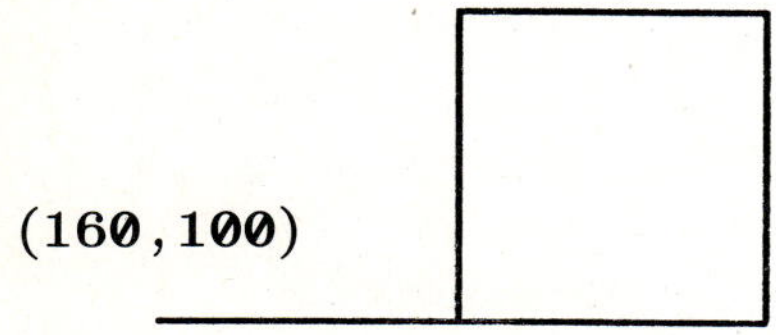

4. Write direct mode statements that will set the following points.

a. The center of the screen.

b. The upper left-hand corner.

---

c. The top center point.

---

d. The point (240,150).

---

5. a. What is the radius of the circle drawn by entering the following direct mode statement?

```
CIRCLE (140,90),30,2
```

---

b. What is the center of this circle?

---

6. Write a direct mode statement that will draw a circle of radius 40 with center at (80,50) and paint it palette color 1.

---

7. a. How do you get into a graphics screen mode?

---

b. How do you allow color to appear in medium resolution graphics mode?

---

8. Which note lasts longest when the following direct mode statement is entered?

```
PLAY "A4 B16 C32"
```

9. Which note is highest when the following direct mode statements are entered?

```
PLAY "02 C8"
PLAY "05 C2"
```

CHAPTER 5

COMPUTER ARITHMETIC AND PROGRAM MANAGEMENT

5–1 OBJECTIVES

Now that you have learned how to turn on your IBM Personal Computer, how to bring up BASICA, and how to communicate with the computer, we are ready to go on to more interesting tasks. You will need a blank diskette for some of these activities.

Arithmetic on the Computer

Ultimately, all mathematics on the computer is done using the simplest arithmetic operations. It is essential to have a clear understanding of how these arithmetic operations are done.

Parentheses ( ) in Computations

As we shall see, all mathematical expressions must be typed on a single line to enter them into the computer. Some expressions can be handled this way only by organizing parts of the expressions in parentheses. Thus, the effective use of parentheses is a necessary skill.

E Notation for Numbers

The computer must deal with both very large and very small numbers. E notation is used by the computer to describe such numbers. We need to be able to recognize and interpret E notation since the computer may type out numbers in this form.

Formatting a Diskette

New or blank diskettes must be prepared or formatted for use on your IBM Personal Computer. We must know how to correctly format diskettes in order to store programs.

Storing and Retrieving Programs

We have already seen some commands. Additional commands will be introduced in this chapter which will permit us to store and retrieve programs using a diskette.

5–2 DISCOVERY EXERCISES

The discovery exercises in this chapter introduce the characteristics of computer arithmetic. In addition, commands for program management will be explored.

Computer Work

1. Turn on your computer and bring up BASICA. Recall from Chapter 2 the following symbols for arithmetic operations:

```
+ Addition
- Subtraction
* Multiplication
/ Division
```

To review the arithmetic operations, type in the following program:

```
100 INPUT A
110 INPUT B
120 LET C = A*B-B/3
130 PRINT C
140 END
```

Display the program and study it briefly. If we execute the program now and enter 2 for **A** and 3 for **B**, what do you think will be typed out?

____

Execute the program and write down what happened.

____

2. Clear out the program in memory. Now type

```
100 LET A = 3*3
110 LET B = 3^2
120 PRINT A
130 PRINT B
140 END
```

Display the program and make sure it is correct. Now execute the program and record what was typed out.

____

Compare the numbers printed out to the expressions in the lines where they were computed. See if you can figure out what is taking place.

3. Type

```
100 LET A = 3*3*3
110 LET B = 3^3
```

Execute the program. What was typed out?

____

4. Type

```
100 LET A = 2*2*2*2
110 LET B = 2^4
```

Execute the program. What was typed out?

____

What is the ^ symbol used for?

____

5. Remember from your introductory algebra course (if you haven't had algebra, don't panic!) that when a number is to be multiplied by itself three times, for example, we can indicate this with an exponent. If the number were 2, we would write the expression as

$$2^3$$

How would this expression be written in BASIC using the ^ symbol? (Hint: see Steps 2, 3, and 4.)

____

6. Fill in the operators (symbols) that call for the following arithmetic operations:

Division

____

Exponentiation

____

Multiplication

____

7. Clear out the program in memory. Type (the AUTO 100 command may be helpful here)

```
100 LET A = 4+2*6/3
110 LET B = (4+2)*6/3
120 LET C = 4+(2*6)/3
130 LET D = 4+2*(6/3)
140 PRINT A
150 PRINT B
160 PRINT C
170 PRINT D
180 END
```

The two points of this program are (1) the order in which the arithmetic is done, and (2) the effect of the parentheses. If you look closely it is clear that the same numbers and operations are involved in each of the calculations in lines 100, 110, 120, and 130. The only difference is the groupings with parentheses in the lines. Execute the program and record what was typed out.

Study the program and the numbers the computer typed out until you see what is taking place in the program. There are very specific rules the computer uses in such situations. We will go over these rules later in the chapter.

---

8. Clear out the program in memory. Now enter the following program:

```
100 LET A = 3*100*100
110 LET B = 3*100*100*100
120 LET C = 3*100*100*100*100
130 PRINT A
140 PRINT B
150 PRINT C
160 END
```

Execute the program and record the output.

Can you explain the different form in which the numbers were typed out? (Hint: Count the number of zeros in the multipliers in lines 100, 110, and 120 in the program.)

9. Type

```
100 LET A = 4/(100*100)
110 LET B = 4/(100*100*100)
120 LET C = 4/(100*100*100*100)
```

Execute the program and record the output.

Again, can you see what is taking place in the output? Count the zeros in the denominators in lines 100,110, and 120.

10. If an E shows up in a number typed out by the computer, what does it mean? Explain in your own words.

____

If you still do not fully understand the purpose of the E notation, don't worry. We will return to it later.

11. Before we can proceed with storing and retrieving programs, we must format a diskette. Type

SYSTEM <ENTER>

to exit the BASICA mode. You will see **A>** on the screen. Diskettes cannot be formatted in the BASICA mode.

12. With the DOS diskette in drive A, type

FORMAT A:/S <ENTER>

After several seconds you will see the message

```
Insert new diskette for drive A:
and strike any key when ready
```

Note: all programs and information stored on this diskette will be lost when the diskette is formatted by striking any key.

13. After removing the DOS diskette and inserting the diskette to be formatted in drive **A**, strike any key when ready.
You will see the message

```
Formatting...
```

After about 35 seconds, you will see

```
Formatting...Format complete
```

and then

```
System transferred
Format another (Y/N)?
```

Type N (Enter is not required here.)
You will see **A>** on the screen.

4. Replace the diskette in drive A with the DOS diskette and bring up BASICA.

5. Replace the DOS diskette with the newly formatted diskette. We are now ready to proceed with storing and retrieving programs.

6. Type

```
FILES <ENTER>
```

You will see displayed on the screen COMMAND .COM as the only program stored on this diskette.

7. Type in the following program

```
100 LET A = 2
110 LET B = 3
120 LET C = A*B
130 PRINT C
140 END
```

8. Display the program to make sure it is correct. Run the program.

9. Now type

```
SAVE"PRODUCT <ENTER>
```

this saves the program in memory onto diskette under the name PRODUCT. Names of programs must be eight characters or less and may be chosen by the reader.

20. Obtain the directory of programs. (See Step 16.) You will see

```
COMMAND .COM PRODUCT .BAS
```

This shows that the program PRODUCT is now on the diskette.

21. Clear out the program in memory by typing

```
NEW <ENTER>
```

Again obtain the directory of programs. (See Step 16.) Are the programs on the diskette affected when the program is cleared out of memory?

____

22. Type in the following program.

```
100 LET D = 2*6-8/4
110 PRINT D
120 END
```

Run the program. Think of a name for this program other than PRODUCT. Again, limit the name to eight or fewer letters of the alphabet. Record the name below.

____

Move the program in memory to diskette under the name you just recorded above. (See Step 19.) Now display the program in memory. Is the program you just saved to diskette still in memory?

____

23. Obtain the directory of programs stored on diskette. Are the two programs you just entered there?

____

Now, we should have two programs stored that were just entered. The name of the first program is PRODUCT; the name of the second was written in Step 22. To simplify the discussion, this second program will be referred to as **program 22**. You, of course, must use the name you selected for the second program.

4. To move PRODUCT from disk to memory, type

```
LOAD"PRODUCT <ENTER>
```

Display this program and verify that it is the right one. Now move **program 22** from disk to memory. Display the program in memory. Which one is there now?

____

What happened to the program PRODUCT that was in memory when we moved **program 22** into memory from diskette?

____

5. Move PRODUCT into memory with the LOAD command. (See Step 24.) Remove the program PRODUCT from diskette by typing

```
KILL"PRODUCT.BAS
```

Display the program in memory. When we cleared out PRODUCT on diskette, did it affect anything in memory?

____

6. Obtain a directory of the programs stored on diskette. PRODUCT should not be there, but **program 22** should be. Inspect the listing of programs. Is everything the way it should be?

____

7. Note that if we now clear out the memory, we will lose both the copy of PRODUCT on diskette (we removed that in Step 25) and the copy in memory. Clear out the memory. (See Step 21.) Display the program in memory. Is anything there?

____

Try to move PRODUCT from disk to memory. (See Step 24.) What happened?

____

Clear out **program 22** from the diskette. (See Step 25.) Turn off the computer.

5–3 DISCUSSION

A number of very important points have been introduced in the computer work. You probably were fairly successful going through the discovery exercises. However, a reasonable understanding of the material to this point is necessary to move smoothly through the rest of the book. Consequently, we will go over each of the objectives of the chapter in great detail to ensure that they are mastered.

Arithmetic on the Computer

We are concerned with five arithmetic operations. These are addition, subtraction, multiplication, division, and exponentiation (+, –, *, /, ^). The first four are certainly familiar to you, and the last (exponentiation) is frightening mainly because of the fierce-looking word used to define the process.

The exponentiation operation is represented by the ^ symbol. Exponentiation merely means "raised to the power." Therefore, 3^4 means "3 raised to the fourth power," which in turn means 3 multiplied by itself four times, giving 81 as the result.

We must be very careful to understand the order in which arithmetic operations are done by the computer. An example will illustrate the point. Consider the following expression:

2+3^2/5–1

If the computer simply goes through the expression from the left, performing operations as they are met, the result would be 2 plus 3 (giving 5), raised to the second power, (giving 25), divided by 5 (giving 5), minus 1 producing an answer of 4. However, suppose addition and subtraction are done first, then exponentiation, then multiplication and division. This would give 5 raised to the second power divided by four. And then 5 raised to the second power (giving 25) divided by four, for an answer of 6.25.

Clearly, we could go on with different rules for the order of arithmetic operations and might get different answers each time. The point is that there are well-defined rules in BASIC for the order and priority of arithmetic operations, and we must understand them. Here they are:

The order of operations is from left to right using the priority rules below.

The priority for arithmetic operations is
1st: Exponentiation
2nd: Multiplication and division
3rd: Addition and subtraction

Now if we go back to our example of

2+3^2/5-1

we scan left to right for any exponentiation. Since there is an exponentiation indicated (3^2), it is done first. Now the expression is

2+9/5-1

Scanning from left to right, we look for exponentiation, and finding none, look for the operations with the next highest priority (multiplication and division). The division is therefore done next, with the following result:

2+1.8-1

Since there are no more multiplications or divisions left in the expression, we scan from left to right for addition and subtraction. The addition gives

3.8-1

and the final subtraction produces the answer of 2.8.

Review the rules for order and priority of arithmetic operations until they become second nature to you. We will look at the rules again when the use of parentheses is discussed in the next section.

Parenthese*s in Computations*

The rules for order and priority of arithmetic operations are not the whole issue, however. There is often a bit more involved. To see this, consider the following more complicated example:

((2*3+4^2)*2+5)*(3^2-4)

The difference between this expression and the ones we have been studying is the use of parentheses to group parts of the expression. We will go through this example in great detail to show you how the computer attacks the arithmetic.

The computer starts by scanning from left to right and meets the left parenthesis of **B**. It then looks inside to see if there are any left parentheses and finds one for **A**. The next parenthesis met is a right parenthesis for **A**. At this point, the computer has isolated the first group of operations to be done. This is

2*3+4^2

and is evaluated using the order and priority rules. The result is 22 (check it). Now our problem has become

(22*2+5)*(3^2-4)

On the next scan, the computer isolates parentheses **B**, does the arithmetic inside, and the problem is now

49*(3^2-4)

Since there are only the (parentheses left, the computer does the arithmetic inside, giving

49*5

which after the final multiplication results in the answer of 245.

Thus, if parentheses are nested the computer works back out from the deepest set, working from left to right. When a set of parentheses is removed, the arithmetic operations inside are done according to the order and priority rules already given. A very good rule of thumb for the beginner to follow is that if there can possibly be any confusion about how the computer will evaluate an expression, use extra parentheses. Too many cannot hurt, but too few certainly can.

E Notation for Numbers

Numbers are printed out by BASIC in different forms. In particular, numbers are sometimes printed out in what is known as the E notation. Examples of the E notation are 2.145E+06 or 6.032E–07. Now we will go back over the ideas introduced in the computer work to clarify the idea of E notation.

It is easy to see why such a special notation is needed for either very large or very small numbers. The computer usually prints out seven digits for a number (Your IBM Personal Computer has the capability of double precision, 16 digits. See your "BASIC" reference manual for additional information). A problem comes up if we want the computer to print out a variable whose value is 45612800000 which would require eleven digits. The computer will print this out as 4.56128E+10, which means that the decimal point belongs ten places to the right of its present position. A variable whose value is 8956000000000 would be printed out as 8.956E+12. The E+12 means that the decimal point belongs twelve places to the right. We can also express very small numbers in the same way. A variable whose value is 0.0000000683 would be typed out as 6.83E–08. The E–08 means that the decimal point belongs eight places to the left. The table below should help you understand how to convert from decimal to E notation or from E notation back to decimal notation.

Decimal Form	E Notation
2630000	2.63E+06
263000	2.63E+05
26300	2.63E+04
2630	2.63E+03
263	2.63E+02
26.3	2.63E+01
2.63	2.63
0.263	2.63E–01
0.0263	2.63E–02
0.00263	2.63E–03
0.000263	2.63E–04
0.0000263	2.63E–05
0.00000263	2.63E–06

To change from E notation to decimal notation, look at the sign following the E. If the number is +, Move the decimal point to the right as many places as the number. If the sign after the E is –, move the decimal point to the left. To convert from decimal to E notation, just reverse the process.

Actually, you shouldn't get very tense about the E notation, since you will rarely use it when setting up programs on the computer. The main reason for bringing up the issue is that the computer may type out numbers in the E notation. Consequently, you should be able to recognize what is happening.

Storing and Retrieving Programs

When we turn off the computer, we lose the program in memory. If every time we turned on the computer, we had to type in programs that we wanted to use, very little work would get done. Fortunately, one of the nice characteristics of the IBM Personal Computer is that we can type in long or complicated programs, troubleshoot them, and then store the programs on a formatted diskette for future use. We need only turn on the computer, bring up BASICA, and then retrieve any of the programs that have been previously stored.

We might not want to keep a specific program on a diskette forever. A command is provided to clear programs from diskette storage . If you move a copy of a program from a diskette into memory and then clear out the copy on the diskette, the copy in memory is not touched. Likewise, you can have one program in memory and clear out another program in diskette storage without changing the first.

The commands for performing these program-management tasks are given below.

TO MOVE A PROGRAM FROM MEMORY
TO DISKETTE STORAGE

TYPE **SAVE"**⟨name of program⟩

TO MOVE A PROGRAM FROM DISK STORAGE
TO MEMORY

TYPE **LOAD"**⟨name of program⟩

TO CLEAR OUT A PROGRAM ON
DISKETTE STORAGE

TYPE **KILL"**⟨name of program⟩.bas

TO DISPLAY A DIRECTORY OF PROGRAMS

TYPE **FILES**

In using the SAVE command, we must be very careful. For instance, if we have just brought up BASICA and wish to move a program to memory, but inadvertently type SAVE" instead of LOAD", then the program on the diskette will be replace by the "program" in memory which has no lines. Thus, we would have destroyed the program we wanted to use. This kind of problem can be avoided if back-up or spare copies of programs are kept on diskette.

5–4 PRACTICE TEST

The practice test that follows is provided for you to check how well you have learned the key points and objectives of the chapter. Check your answers against the key given at the end of the book.

1. Write down the symbols that are used to carry out the following arithmetic operations in BASIC expressions:

a. Multiplication

____

b. Exponentiation

____

c. Division

____

2. When evaluating arithmetic expressions, there is a priority of operations. What is this priority?

a. 1st

____

b. 2nd

____

c. 3rd

____

3. When scanning arithmetic expressions, the computer searches in a specific direction. What is this direction

____

4. Write a BASIC statement to evaluate the following expression. Number the line 100.

$$A = (4 + 3B/D)^2$$

____

5. If the following program is executed, what will be typed out?

```
100 LET A = 2
110 LET B = 3
120 LET C = (A*B+2)/2
130 PRINT C
140 END
```

6. Convert the following numbers to E notation:

a. 5160000

b. 0.0000314

7. Convert the following numbers to decimal notation.

a. 7.258E+06

b. 1.437E–03

8. In the expression below, give the order in which the operations will be done by the computer.

```
100 LET A = (6/3+4)^2
```

9. What commands are needed to carry out the following operations:

a. Move a program from disk storage to memory.

b. Move a program from memory to disk storage.

c. Clear out a program in disk storage.

d. Clear out a program in memory.

e. Display the program in memory.

f. Execute the program in memory.

g. Display the names of all the files saved on diskette.

10. Suppose you are typing a line into the computer and have not yet pressed ENTER. How do you correct a single character?

CHAPTER 6

INPUT, OUTPUT, AND SIMPLE APPLICATIONS

6–1 OBJECTIVES

In this chapter we will get down to the business of writing programs. We will also increase our knowledge of BASIC by looking at some details about input and output. The objectives are as follows.

Getting Numbers into a BASIC program

There are only three ways that we can enter numbers into the computer for a BASIC program. Since the computer is concerned mainly with numbers, we need to understand how to input these numbers.

Printing Out Variables and Strings

After information is computed, it must be printed out. Different choices are available for the kind of output. Usually we will want to output strings of characters as well as numbers. This string output is handled essentially the same as numbers, but needs special attention.

Spacing the Printout

The previous objective is concerned with the output of numbers and strings of characters. Here we are concerned with the spacing of that output.

The REMARK Statement

The wise programmer includes comments in programs to help explain or interpret what is being done. The REMARK statement in BASIC permits us to do this.

Simple Applications

Our ultimate goal is to learn how to write and troubleshoot programs. In this chapter we will begin with some modest program assignments.

6–2 DISCOVERY EXERCISES

The necessary preliminary details have already been seen to. Therefore, we can proceed directly to the computer work to explore the objectives of the chapter.

Computer Work

1. Turn on the computer and bring up BASICA. Enter the following program:

```
100 INPUT A
110 INPUT B
120 INPUT C
130 LET D = A+B+C
140 PRINT D
150 END
```

What do you think will happen if we execute this program?

____

Execute the program. When the first question mark is typed out (the INPUT prompt for A), type in 2. Likewise, when the second question mark comes up, type in 3, and finally, at the last question mark, type in 5. Record what happened below.

____

2. Note that in the program in Step 1 we have three INPUT statements (lines 100, 110, and 120). Type

```
100
110
```

What does this do to the program?

Display the program in memory and see if you are right. Then type

```
120 INPUT A,B,C
```

Display the program. What has happened?

---

3. Execute the program and when the INPUT prompt (?) is output, type in

```
2,3,5
```

What happened?

Can you input more than one variable at a time in a BASIC program?

---

4. Execute the program, and when the INPUT prompt is output, type

```
2,3
```

What happened?

What is the computer waiting for?

Type

```
2,3,5
```

and record below what happened.

---

5. Execute the program and when the INPUT prompt appears, type

```
2,3,5,1
```

What happened?

____

Type

```
2,3,5
```

and record what happened below.

____

6. Can you type in more numbers than called for at an INPUT statement?

____

What will happen if you do?

____

7. Can you type in fewer numbers than called for at an INPUT statement?

____

What will happen if you do?

____

8. Type

```
120 READ A,B,C
```

Display the program. What has happened?

____

Execute the program and record what happened.

9. Now type

```
125 DATA 2,3,5
```

and display the program. What has happened?

0. Execute the program and record what happened.

Based upon what you have just seen, anytime a BASIC program contains a READ statement, there must be another type of statement in the program. What is that statement?

1. Name two different methods (other than using a LET statement) for getting numbers into a program. (Hint: See Steps 2 and 8.)

2. Display the program in memory. Delete the DATA statement. Type

```
145 DATA 2,3,5
```

and display the program again. What has happened?

3. Execute the program and record the output.

Does it appear to make any difference where the DATA statement is in the program?

____

14. Clear out the program in memory. Enter the program below

```
100 READ A,B
110 LET C = A/B
120 PRINT C
130 GOTO 100
140 DATA 2,1,6,2,90,9,35,7
150 END
```

What do you think will happen if you execute the program?

____

Try it and see if you were correct. Record the output.

____

Is the "out of data" message associated with the READ statement or the DATA statement?

____

15. Delete the DATA statement in line 140 from the program. Now enter the following statements:

```
105 DATA 10,2
115 DATA 100,50
125 DATA 50,5
```

Display the program in memory. What has taken place?

____

16. If we execute the program, what do you think will be displayed?

____

Execute the program and see if you were correct. Record the output below.

____

7. Can you have more than one DATA statement in a BASIC program?

____

Does it seem to make any difference where the DATA statements are in the program?

____

8. Clear out the program in memory. Enter the following program:

```
100 LET A = 10
110 PRINT A
120 END
```

What will happen if you execute this program?

____

Execute the program and record what took place.

____

9. Now type

```
110 PRINT "A"
```

and display the program in memory. What has happened?

____

What will happen if we execute the program?

____

Execute the program and record what the computer typed out.

____

20. Type

```
110 PRINT "HOUND DOG = ";A
```

and display the program in memory. What do you think will happen if we execute this program?

____

Execute the program and record what did happen.

____

21. Now let's try a different wrinkle. Type

```
110 PRINT "B = ";A
```

Display the program and study it carefully. If we execute the program, what do you think will happen?

____

Try it and see if you were right. Record the output below.

____

22. Type

```
95 REM DEMO PROGRAM
```

Display the program. What has happened?

____

Execute the program. What was the output?

____

Does the REM statement in line 95 have any effect on the program?

____

3. Clear out the program in memory. Enter the following program:

```
100 REM METRIC CONVERSION PROGRAM
110 REM CONVERT LBS TO GRAMS
120 PRINT "INPUT NO. OF LBS.";
130 INPUT P
140 LET G = 454*P
150 PRINT P;" POUNDS IS ";G;"GRAMS"
160 GOTO 120
170 END
```

Display the program and verify it is correct. Study the program carefully and try to guess what will happen if it is executed. Now execute the program. When the INPUT prompt is typed out, enter any number you desire. Note what is typed out. Repeat this process several times, then jump the computer out of the INPUT loop. If you have forgotten how, see Chapter 3, Step 22 of the computer work. What is the purpose of the REM statement?

____

4. Type

```
115 INPUT P
130
160 GOTO 115
```

and then display the program in memory. What has happened?

____

Will the program work in this form?

____

Execute the program and at the INPUT prompt, type 1. What happened?

____

Jump the program out of the INPUT loop.

25. Let's experiment with this program a bit more. Clear out the program in memory and enter it again, modified as follows:

```
100 REM METRIC CONVERSION PROGRAM
110 REM CONVERT LBS. TO GRAMS
120 PRINT "INPUT NO. OF LBS.";
130 INPUT P
140 PRINT P;"POUNDS IS ";G;"GRAMS"
150 LET G = 454*P
160 GOTO 120
170 END
```

Can the program be executed in this form?

____

Execute the program and at the INPUT prompt, type 2. What happened?

____

Explain in your own words what is wrong. Remember that if a variable is not defined initially in your program, your computer will set it equal to 0.

____

Jump the program out of the INPUT loop.

26. Clear out the program in memory. Enter the following program:

```
100 READ A
110 PRINT A
120 GOTO 100
130 DATA 10,12,8,9,73,60,82
140 END
```

Execute the program and record what happened.

____

7. Type

```
110 PRINT A,
```

Note that all we have done is to insert a comma after the A in line 110. Execute the program and record what happened.

____

8. Now replace the comma after A with a semicolon by typing

```
110 PRINT A;
```

Execute the program and record what happened.

____

9. If a variable in a PRINT statement is not followed by any punctuation marks, what happens after the number is printed out? (Hint: See Step 26.)

____

Suppose the variable is followed by a comma?

____

What will happen if the variable is followed by a semicolon?

____

0. Clear out the program in memory and enter the following program:

```
100 LET A = 20
110 READ B
120 PRINT TAB(A);B;
130 LET A = A+10
140 GOTO 110
150 DATA 1,2,3
160 END
```

Execute the program and record what happened.

____

31. Type

```
130 LET A = A+5
```

Execute the program and record what happened.

____

32. Type

```
130 LET A = A+20
```

Execute the program and record what happened.

____

33. What does the TAB in the print statement appear to control?

____

34. This concludes the computer work for now. Turn off the computer.

6–3 DISCUSSION

In this chapter we have begun to get away from the mere mechanics of controlling the computer. Instead, we now concentrate more on writing and troubleshooting programs. This skill doesn't come naturally to most people, and consequently we will give the topic a great deal of attention, both now and in later chapters.

Getting Numbers into a BASIC Program

In Chapter 2 we saw one way to get numbers into a program. That was by assigning values to a variable in the program itself. For example,

```
100 LET A = 6
```

introduces the value 6 into a program and stores the number under the variable name A. This method has limitations. We need to examine other ways in which numbers can be introduced into a

BASIC program. Let's look first at the INPUT statement and how it is used. An example might be

```
260 INPUT G
```

When the computer executes this line, it will type out a question mark as a prompt that input is expected from the terminal, then will halt and wait for you to type in the number. In the case above, the number typed in will be known as G.

More than one variable may be called for in a single INPUT statement, such as

```
420 INPUT A,B,C,D
```

In this case the same INPUT prompt (the question mark) is typed out, but now the computer is expecting four numbers to be typed in, separated by commas. If only three numbers (or less) are entered and the ENTER key pressed, the computer will type **Redo from start**. If more than four numbers are typed in initially, the same message will appear.

The last method of providing for numerical input into the computer is with the READ and DATA statements. The statement

```
100 READ A,B,C,D
```

is handled by the computer the same as the INPUT statement with two exceptions. First, the computer does not stop. There is no need to, as will be seen. The second exception is that the numbers called for are read from DATA statements contained within the program rather than being entered at the terminal in response to an INPUT prompt.

To illustrate the READ and DATA statements, consider the following program:

```
100 READ A,B,C,D
110 LET E = A+B+C+D
120 PRINT E
130 DATA 25,3,17,12
140 END
```

The program reads four numbers from the DATA statement and prints out the sum of the numbers. It makes no difference where the DATA statement is in the program. There can be more than one DATA statement, and they need not be grouped together at the same place in the program. As numbers are called for by READ statements, they are taken in order from the DATA statements, beginning with the lowest numbered statement. Should numbers be requested after all have been used from the available DATA statements, the computer will type an "out of data" message and then halt.

To sum up, there are three methods by which numbers can be introduced into BASIC programs. They are using (1) LET statements, (2) the INPUT statement, and (3) the READ and DATA statements. There are times when each of these methods can be used to advantage. You will become familiar with the advantages and disadvantages of each method as we spend more time writing programs.

■ **You can put numbers in a BASIC program with:**
1) LET (assignment)
2) READ-DATA
3) INPUT

Printing Out Variables and Strings

Output from the computer is quite simple. The computer can print out either the numerical value of a variable (a number) or a string of characters. To illustrate, suppose we have a variable named X and the number 2 is stored in that location. The program

```
100 LET X = 2
110 PRINT "X"
120 PRINT X
130 END
```

shows the difference between string and variable output. Line 110 prints out the character X since X is enclosed in quotation marks. Line 120 prints 2 since that is the number stored in location X.

The rule is clear. Any characters contained within quotation marks are called strings. Strings are printed out exactly as listed. The computer does not attempt to analyze or detect what is in the strings. If a variable in a PRINT statement is not contained within quotes, the computer prints out the numerical value of that variable.

It is possible to do computation within a PRINT statment. Thus

```
100 PRINT A+B+C,D
```

will cause the computer to print out the sum of the numbers stored in A, B, and C, then the number stored in D. Of course, the variables A, B, C, and D would have to be previously defined or the computer will assign zeros for their values.

Spacing the Printout

BASIC has a "built-in" standard spacing mechanism that prints six numbers spaced equally on one line (or five with older versions of BASICA). Where possible, this standard spacing is used by the computer when quantities in a PRINT statement are separated by commas. The comma signals the computer to move to the next print position on the line. If the computer is already at the last position on a line and encounters a comma in a PRINT statement, it does a carriage return and prints the number on the first position on the next line. Thus

```
100 PRINT A,B,C,D,E,F,G
```

would cause the numerical values of A, B, C, D, E, and F to be printed evenly spaced across a line in the six standard positions. The numerical value of F would be printed below the value of A on the next line.

■ **Commas in PRINT statements produce 6 columns per line.**

Another type of spacing is produced by the semicolon between variables such as

```
100 PRINT A;B;C
```

The semicolon produces closer spacing than the standard spacing obtained with the comma. However, the spacing is not always uniform, since numbers may be typed out in different formats.

We will let it go with the statement that

```
100 PRINT A;B
```

produces closer spacing of output than

```
100 PRINT A,B
```

Finally, we can control the spacing on a line in great detail by using the TAB function in PRINT statements. The TAB function works the same way as a tabulator setting on a typewriter. There are eighty tab positions available on the screen.

The statement

```
100 PRINT TAB(15);A;TAB(32);B
```

signals the computer to space over to the fifteenth printing position, print the numerical value of A, space over to the thirty-second printing position, and finally print the numerical value of B. It is also possible to have a variable tab setting that is controlled by the computer:

```
100 PRINT TAB(X);A
```

Here the computer must first look up the value of X, then space over to the printing position determined by the largest integer in X (for example, if X= 23.1435, the computer will space over to the twenty-third printing position), then print out the numerical value of A.

■ **Use the TAB function to produce variable spacing.**

One final comment about the PRINT statement. We can produce vertical spacing in the output by using an empty PRINT statment as follows:

```
100 PRINT
```

The computer looks for the quantity to be printed and finds none. It then looks for punctuation, and finding none, orders a carriage return and advances the paper one line. If we wanted two or three empty lines in the printout, we can obtain the spacing by using as many empty PRINT statements as desired.

The REMARK Statement

The REM (stands for "remark") statement is quite different from the statements we have seen previously. As soon as the computer senses the characters REM following the line number, it ignores the balance of the statement and goes on to the next line. What, then, is the purpose of the REM statement if the computer pays no attention to it? The REM statement is a way of providing information for the benefit of the programmer or someone reading the program. This information makes it much easier to follow what is taking place in the program. The wise programmer will use REM statements liberally.

To illustrate the use of the REM statements, two programs will be presented. They both will produce identical results, but the second uses REM statements to describe what is happening in the program. You can be the judge of which program is easier to follow.

1. No REM statements:

```
100 INPUT A,B,C,D,
110 LET X = (A+B+C+D)/4
120 PRINT X
130 END
```

2. With REM statements:

```
100 REM COMPUTE THE AVERAGE OF FOUR NUMBERS
110 REM INPUT THE FOUR NUMBERS
120 INPUT A,B,C,D
130 REM COMPUTE THE AVERAGE
140 LET X = (A+B+C+D)/4
150 REM PRINT OUT THE AVERAGE
160 PRINT X
170 END
```

■ **Put information in a program with a REM statement.**

6—4 PROGRAM EXAMPLES

As we said, we will spend progressively more time writing and debugging programs. The examples chosen for this chapter are very simple but illustrate the ideas we have been discussing. Study each example carefully until you are certain you understand all the details. You might want to enter the programs into the computer and execute them to verify they work as intended.

Example 1 - Unit Prices

Our problem is to write a program to compute unit prices on supermarket items. We will let T stand for the total price, N for the number of items, and U for the unit price. We can compute the unit price with the following relationship:

$$U = T/N$$

As an example, suppose that a case of twelve large cans of fruit juice costs $6.96. The unit cost per can would be

$$U = 6.96/12 = \$0.58$$

We want the program to be designd so that when executed it will produce the following output:

WHAT IS THE TOTAL PRICE? (You enter value of T)
WHAT IS THE NUMBER OF ITEMS? (You enter value of N)
UNIT PRICE IS (Computer types out value of U)

Now we will break this example apart to see how the program is related to what we want to see in the output.

WHAT IS THE TOTAL PRICE? (Entry of T)
  100 200
WHAT IS THE NUMBER OF ITEMS? (Entry of N)
  300 400
500: Compute unit price.
UNIT PRICE IS (Output of U)
  600 700

We will write each line of the program so that the numbers below will be the line numbers in the program. In line 100 we want the computer to type out the message indicated. This is done with the PRINT command.

```
100 PRINT "WHAT IS THE TOTAL PRICE? ";
```

Note the semicolon outside the closing quotation marks. The reason for this is that we do not want to get a carriage return but instead want the printed line to hold there for the INPUT prompt. Line 200 should be an INPUT statement to call for the input of T.

```
200 INPUT T
```

The message in line 300 requires a PRINT statement.

```
300 PRINT "WHAT IS THE NUMBER OF ITEMS? ";
```

The input for the total number of items is handled the same as the total price.

```
400 INPUT N
```

Next we compute the unit price in line 500.

```
500 LET U = T/N
```

The next line is a message, followed by the unit price, and is handled with a PRINT statement.

```
600 PRINT "UNIT PRICE IS ";U
```

Finally, we have an END statement.

```
700 END
```

Now we pull the whole program together.

```
100 PRINT "WHAT IS THE TOTAL PRICE? ";
200 INPUT T
300 PRINT "WHAT IS THE NUMBER OF ITEMS? ";
400 INPUT N
500 LET U = T/N
600 PRINT "UNIT PRICE IS ";U
700 END
```

Study the program to make sure you see the purpose of each line as related to the original statement of the problem.

Example 2 - Converting Temperature

The relationship between temperature measured in degrees Fahrenheit and in degrees Celsius is

$$C = (5/9)(F - 32)$$

Let C stand for degrees Celsisus and F stand for degrees Fahrenheit. If, for example, F is 212, then C is determined to be

$$C = (5/9)(212 - 32) = 100$$

As in the first example, we will write the program after seeing how we want the output to appear. Let's suppose that if we execute the desired program, we want to see the following:

```
INPUT NO. OF DEGREES F
?  (You enter value of F)
(Value of F) DEGREES F IS (answer) DEGREES C
```

Again we will split the output up into parts that will be generated by the lines in the program:

```
INPUT NO. OF DEGREES F
          100
200: Entry of F
300: Compute degrees C
(Output of F) DEGREES F IS (Output of C) DEGREES C
          400
```

The corresponding program is

```
100 PRINT "INPUT NO. OF DEGREES F "
200 INPUT F
300 LET C = (5/9)*(F - 32)
400 PRINT F;" DEGREES F IS ";C;" DEGREES C"
500 END
```

This program is a bit different from the first example. In line 100 there is no puncuation following the string. Thus the INPUT prompt generated by the INPUT statement in line 200 will be printed out on the line following the initial string. The PRINT statement in line 400 prints out (1) the value of F, (2) a string, (3) the value of C, and (4) a second string. The semicolons in line 400 are used to set off the variables and strings in the PRINT statements.

Example 3 - Sum and Product of Numbers

The final example in this chapter will be concerned with the computation of the sum and product of two numbers. Again we will write the program to get the desired output. In this case, when the program is executed, we want to see

> **INPUT A?** (You enter value of A)
> **INPUT B?** (You enter value of B)
> **SUM OF A AND B IS** (Computer prints out sum)
> **PRODUCT OF A AND B IS** (Computer prints out product)
> (Blank lines are inserted by the computer.)
> **INPUT A?** (You enter value of A)
> (etc.)

Since we broke the first two examples apart in great detail, we can proceed more rapidly with this problem. The first line of the desired output can be handled by the following two statements:

```
100 PRINT "INPUT A ";
110 INPUT A
```

Note carefully that the message printed out in line 100 is window dressing for the program and has nothing to do with the actual calculations. The input instruction that is important to the computer is in line 110. We generate the second line of the desired output as follows:

```
120 PRINT "INPUT B ";
130 INPUT B
```

The sum and product of the two numbers are printed out as follows:

```
140 PRINT "SUM OF A AND B IS ";A+B
150 PRINT "PRODUCT OF A AND B IS ";A*B
```

The spacing between the output of the original set of numbers and that obtained when the program loops back, as well as the looping instructions, can be obtained with three statements.

```
160 PRINT
170 PRINT
180 GOTO 100
```

Of course, the final line should be the END statement.

```
190 END
```

The whole program is listed below.

```
100 PRINT "INPUT A ";
110 INPUT A
120 PRINT "INPUT B ";
130 INPUT B
140 PRINT "SUM OF A AND B IS ";A+B
150 PRINT "PRODUCT OF A AND B IS ";A*B
160 PRINT
170 PRINT
180 GOTO 100
190 END
```

As structured, the program will keep looping back until we jump the program out of the INPUT loop. We could have computed the sum and product of the two numbers in separate lines, as in the following version of the same program.

```
100 PRINT "INPUT A ";
110 INPUT A
120 PRINT "INPUT B ";
130 INPUT B
140 LET S = A+B
150 PRINT "SUM OF A AND B IS ";S
160 LET P = A*B
170 PRINT "PRODUCT OF A AND B IS ";P
180 PRINT
190 PRINT
200 GOTO 100
210 END
```

6–5 PROBLEMS

1. Write a program that will read the four numbers 10, 9, 1, and 2 from a DATA statement, putting the numbers in A, B, C, and D, respectively. Add the first two numbers putting the sum in S. Then compute the product of the last two numbers, putting the result in P. Print out the value of S and P on the same line.

2. Write a program that will call for the input of four numbers, then print back the numbers in reverse order. For example, if you type in 5, 2, 11, 12, the computer should type back 12, 11, 2, 5. The program must work for any set of four numbers that you decide to type in. Oh yes, you can use only three lines in your program.

3. Write a program to read variables A, B, C, and D from numbers of your choice in a DATA statement. Print out the numbers vertically with B below A, C below B, and D below C.

4. What will be output if we execute the following program?

```
100 READ X,Y,Z
110 DATA 2,5,3
120 LET T = X*Y+Z
130 LET S = Y^2
140 PRINT T,S
150 END
```

5. What is wrong with this program?

```
100 LET A = 2
110 READ B
120 LET A = A+C/B
130 DATA 3
140 PRINT A
150 END
```

6. Explain in your own words what the following program does.

```
100 INPUT A,B
110 LET S = A+B
120 LET T = A-B
130 LET U = A*B
140 PRINT S,T,U
150 END
```

7. One of the ratios used to judge the health of a business is the acid-test ratio. The acid-test ratio is the sum of cash, marketable securities, and receivables, the sum divided by current liabilities. Write a program to call for the input of the necessary quantities, then compute and output the acid-test ratio.

8. Write a program to count and print out by fives beginning with 0. The first few numbers will be 0, 5, 10, 15, and so on. Interrupt the program manually when forty or fifty numbers have been printed out.

9. The intended output of the program below is 1, 3, 5, 7, 9, and so forth. The program below has an error. What is wrong?

```
100 LET A = 1
110 PRINT A;
120 LET A = A+2
130 GOTO 100
140 END
```

If an object is dropped near the surface of the earth, the distance it will fall in a given time can be determined by

$$S = 16T^2$$

where S is the distance fallen (in feet) and T is the time of fall in seconds. Write a program that, when executed, will produce the following output:

TIME OF FALL (SEC) ? (You enter T)
OBJECT FALLS (Computer types out S) **FEET**

The volume of a box can be computed as

$$V = LWH$$

where L, W, H are the length, width and height, respectively. If these are all measured in centimeters, for example, the volume will be in cubic centimeters. We want a program that will produce the following output when executed:

LENGTH (CM) ? (You enter L)
WIDTH (CM) ? (You enter W)
HEIGHT (CM) ? (You enter H)
VOLUME IS (Computer types out V) **CUBIC CM.**

The program below is incorrect and will not produce the output called for above. What is wrong?

```
100 PRINT "LENGTH (CM)";L
110 PRINT "WIDTH (CM)";W
120 PRINT "HEIGHT (CM)";H
130 INPUT L,W,H
140 LET V = L*W*H
150 PRINT "VOLUME IS"
160 PRINT V
170 PRINT "CUBIC CM."
180 END
```

12. In the program below two numbers, A and B, are called for in the INPUT statement. The problem is to supply the missing statements so that when A and B are printed out, the values have been interchanged.

```
100 INPUT A,B
110
120
130
140 PRINT A,B
150 END
```

13. Suppose the odometer on your car reads R_1 miles when the gas tank is full. You drive until the odometer reading is R_2 at which point G gallons of gasoline are required to fill the tank. The miles per gallon you got on the drive is

$$M = (R_2 - R_1)/G$$

Write a program to figure out the mileage for the following data:

R_1	R_2	G
21423	21493	5
05270	05504	13
65214	65559	11.5

14. Let's suppose you are writing a program to print out numbers on a form. Assume that there are three numbers to be handled and they are in a DATA statement. Write a program which will print the first number beginning 20 characters in from the left of the output device. Follow this with two blank lines. Print the second number beginning at character 10. Print a blank line followed by the third number beginning at character 15. Put any numbers you wish in the DATA statement and try out the program.

15. It is known that a DATA statement contains examination grades for a class of ten students. Write a program containing no more than four statements counting the DATA and END statement to compute and print out the class average. Try out the program on sample data of your choice.

6. There is an old tale of a wise man who invented the game of chess and as a reward asked to receive 1 grain of wheat on the first square of the chess board, 2 grains on the second, 4 grains on the third, 8 on the fourth, and so on. Write a program to print out the number of the square and the number of grains on that square. The program should involve a loop using a GOTO statement and should be interrupted at the keyboard when you have seen enough. How many grains of wheat will be on the 64th square? RUN the program and find out.

7. If compound interest is paid, the true annual interest rate is higher than the nominal rate which is quoted for the investment. The following BASIC formula computes this true annual interest rate:

```
T = ((1+R/(100*M))^M-1)*100
```

In this expression, T is the true annual interest rate in percent, R is the nominal interest rate in percent, and M is the number of times the investment is compounded per year. Write a program which will produce the following output when executed:

QUOTED INTEREST RATE (PERCENT)
? (type in at keyboard)
NUMBER OF TIMES COMPOUNDED PER YEAR
? (type in at keyboard)
TRUE ANNUAL INTEREST RATE IS
(computer types out answer)

8. Simple interest on an investment is computed according to the following rule:

$$I = (P)(R/100)(T/365)$$

where P is the principal invested at an annual interest rate R (expressed in percent) for a time T (expressed in days). Write a program which will generate the display shown below when executed.

```
WHAT IS THE PRINCIPAL
?  (type in the principal at the keyboard)
WHAT IS THE ANNUAL INTEREST RATE (%)
?  (type in the interest rate at the keyboard)
WHAT IS THE TERM IN DAYS
?  (type in the term at the keyboard)

FOR AN INVESTMENT OF
(Computer types out the principal)
AT AN ANNUAL INTEREST RATE OF
(Computer types out the rate)
PERCENT INVESTED FOR
(Computer types out the term)
DAYS, THE INTEREST IS
(Computer types out the interest)
```

19. If an amount of money P is left to accumulate interest at a rate of I percent per year for N years, the money will grow to a total amount T given by

T = P*(1+I/100)^N

As an example, if P = $1000, I = 6 percent, and N = 5 years,

T = 1000*(1+6/100)^5 = 1338.23

Write a program that when executed will produce the following output:

```
INITIAL INVESTMENT ?  (You enter P)
ANNUAL INTEREST RATE (%) ?  (You enter I)
YEARS LEFT TO ACCRUE INTEREST ?  (You enter N)
TOTAL VALUE IS (Computer types out T)
```

20. If an amount of money P is left to accumulate interest at I percent compounded J times per year for N years, the value of the investment will be

T = P*(1+I/(100*J))^(J*N)

Write a program that will call for the input of P, I, J and N. Execute the program as needed to get the value of $1000 invested at 8 percent for 2 years compounded

a. Annually (J = 1)
b. Semiannually (J = 2)
c. Monthly (J = 12)
d. Weekly (J = 52)
e. Daily (J = 365)

If a savings and loan company makes a big advertising production about computing the interest every day instead of each week, should you get excited?

6–6 PRACTICE TEST

The practice test that follows is provided for you to check how well you have mastered the key points and objectives of the chapter. Check your answer against the key given at the end of the book.

1. What will be output if the following program is executed?

```
100 LET X = 1
110 PRINT X,
120 LET X = X+1
130 GOTO 110
140 END
```

2. Describe three ways that numbers can be brought into a BASIC program.

3. In a PRINT statement, what is a collection of characters between quotation marks called?

4. What is the purpose of the REM statement?

____

5. If there is a READ statement in a BASIC program, what other type of statement must also be present in the program?

____

6. What will happen if the following program is executed?

```
100 LET X = 3
110 LET Y = 4
120 PRINT "Y = ";X
130 END
```

____

7. How many standard print columns per line are provided for in BASIC when the print quantities are separated by commas?

____

8. How many DATA statements may there be in a program?

____

9. What is the TAB function used for in BASIC?

____

10. What will the output look like if the following program is executed?

```
100 LET A = 1
110 LET B = 3
120 PRINT A,B
130 PRINT A;B
140 END
```

____

1. The program

```
100 INPUT A,B
110 LET C = A+B
120 PRINT C
130 END
```

is executed, and in response to the INPUT prompt you type the numbers 10, 12, and 13. Describe exactly what will happen.

---

2. Miles can be converted to kilometers by multiplying by 1.609. Thus, 10 miles equals 16.09 kilometers, and so on. Write a program that will produce the following printout when executed.

INPUT NO OF MILES? (You type in a number)
(Computer types your number) **MILES EQUAL** (Answer)
KILOMETERS

CHAPTER 7

DECISIONS, BRANCHING, AND APPLICATIONS

7—1 OBJECTIVES

The power of the computer rests in large part on its ability to make decisions about quanitites in programs. In this chapter we will explore this cabability and will go on with the continuing task of learning to program in BASIC, the objectives are as follows.

Making Decisions in Programs

Decisions made in programs can cause the computer to jump to line numbers out of numerical order. Such a transfer to a program line may be unconditional or may depend upon values of variables in the program. The effective use of these conditional and unconditional transfer statements makes simple programs produce powerful and useful results.

Program Applications

As in the previous chapter, we will go on learning how to apply the techniques we study to BASIC programs.

Finding Errors in Programs

Almost all programs have errors in them when first written. Troubleshooting programs is a vital skill that, like programming itself, can be learned.

7–2 DISCOVERY EXERCISES

Computer Work

1. Turn on the computer, bring up BASICA and enter the following program:

```
100 LET X = 1
110 PRINT X
120 LET X = X+1
130 IF X < 5 THEN 110
140 END
```

The < symbol in line 130 means "less than"; thus, the statement translates as "If X is less than 5 then 110." Study the program carefully. What do you think will be printed out if you execute the program?

Execute the program and record what did happen.

2. Now type

```
100 LET X = 2
```

Display the program in memory. What will the output be now?

Execute the program and write down what the computer printed out.

3. Now let's make another change in the program to see if you are following what is taking place. Type

```
120 LET X = X+2
```

Display the program and study it carefully. What do you think the program will do now?

Execute the program and see if you were right. Copy below what actually took place.

4. We want to explore another idea in connection with the program you have in memory, but need to make some changes. If desired, you can modify the program to make it agree with the one below or clear out the program in memory and enter the one below.

```
100 LET X = 1
110 PRINT X
120 LET X = X+1
130 IF X >= 5 THEN 140
135 GOTO 110
140 END
```

Execute the program and record what happened.

Compare the output recorded above to that you copied down in Step 1. Is there any connection?

5. Display the program in memory. In this program there is an assertion stated in line 130. The assertion is X ⟩ = 5, which is read as "X is greater than or equal to 5." If for example, X had the numerical value 6, the assertion would be true. If X had the value 3, the assertion would be false.

   Now suppose we look at the program in Step 4. If the program is executed, the computer starts with line 100, then goes to lines 110, 120, and 130. If the assertion in line 130 is true, which line number will the computer execute next?

   ____

6. Only two conditions have been used so far in the programs. They are

   ⟨ (Less than)
   ⟩ = (Greater than or equal to)

   How would you write the conditions for

   Greater than

   ____

   Less than or equal to

   ____

   Equal to

   ____

   Not equal to

   ____

   If you can fill in the blanks above without too much trouble, fine. If not, don't worry, as we will review everything later. The important thing now is how the IF THEN statement works.

7. Now on to some applications using IF THEN statements. Clear out the program in memory and enter the following program:

```
100 PRINT "INPUT EITHER 1, 2, OR 3 ";
110 INPUT Y
120 IF Y = 1 THEN 150
130 IF Y = 2 THEN 170
140 IF Y = 3 THEN 190
150 PRINT "BLOOD"
160 GOTO 100
170 PRINT "SWEAT"
180 GOTO 100
190 PRINT "TEARS"
200 GOTO 100
210 END
```

Display the program and check that you have entered it correctly. Study the program briefly. Remember that when the program is executed and the computer types out the INPUT prompt, you are supposed to type in either, 1, 2, or 3. Which value of Y will let the computer reach line 120 in the program?

Which value or values of Y will let the computer reach line 130?

How about line 140?

8. Suppose you wanted the computer to type out "SWEAT". What value of Y should be entered?

See if you were right. Execute the program and enter the number you wrote down. What happened?

9. What value of Y will cause the computer to type out BLOOD?

How about making the computer type out TEARS?

____

Check each of the responses you made above to see if you were right.

10. The program assumes that either 1, 2, or 3 will be typed in at the INPUT prompt. Think about the program a bit, then try to figure out what will happen if we type in 4 in response to the input prompt. What do you think will happen?

____

Execute the program, type in 4 in response to the input prompt, and record below what happened.

____

You can easily explain what happened in the program by considering what the computer does when it encounters an assertion in the IF THEN statement. Remember, if the assertion is true, the computer goes to the line number following the THEN. If the condition is false, the computer goes to the next higher line number. Now jump the computer out of the INPUT loop.

11. Let's look at interrupting a program with a single keystroke. Clear out the program in memory and type in the following program:

```
100 LET A$ = INKEY$
110 IF A$ = "Q" THEN 150
120 PRINT "PRESS A KEY.",
130 PRINT A$
140 GOTO 100
150 PRINT "QUIT"
160 END
```

As you run the program, press and hold down several keys before you enter capital Q. Run the program. What happened?

____

Press and release various keys. How many times is each key character displayed?

Press Q to stop the program. Is Q printed out by line 130?

---

2. We will now use another form of the IF THEN statement. Change the program as follows. Delete lines 130 and 150. Change line 110 as follows.

```
110 IF A$ = "" THEN 100 ELSE PRINT A$
```

Run the program. Press several keys. What happens after each key is pressed?

Does the computer indicate that it is awaiting a keystroke?

Press the spacebar several times. Then press K. Does the spacebar create spaces?

Interrupt the program with Ctrl-Break.

3. Delete line 160, the END statement. Now change line 120 of the program as follows:

```
120 IF A$ = "Q" THEN END ELSE 100
```

Before you run this program, what key will you press to end execution? Run the program. Were you right?

Use the EDIT command to replace the Q in line 120 with a space as follows:

```
120 IF A$ = " " THEN END ELSE 100
```

What key will cause the program to end now?

______

Display the program. Now run the program and press several keys before you press the spacebar. Were you right?

______

14. Now let's look at a use of the INKEY$ statement in a graphics program. Clear out the memory, switch to graphics mode (See Chapter 4, Step 1 of the Discovery Exercises, or Appendix A) and type in the following program. (Recall the AUTO 100 command.)

```
100 CLS
110 SCREEN 1
120 LET A = 160
130 LET B = 100
140 PSET (A,B)
150 LET A$ = INKEY$
160 PSET (A,B)
170 PRESET (A,B)
180 IF A$ = "D" THEN B = B+5
190 IF A$ = "U" THEN B = B-5
200 IF A$ = "L" THEN A = A-5
210 IF A$ = "R" THEN A = A+5
220 IF A$ = "Q" THEN END ELSE 150
```

15. This program allows a point to be moved around the screen using the keys marked U, D, L, and R. These capital letters can be typed using the shift key (⇧) or by pressing the Caps Lock key. Use these keys to move the point to the upper left-hand corner of the screen. Can you move the point off the screen?

______

Can you move the point back on the screen?

____

How far does the point move each time U, D, L, or R is pressed? (Listing the program may be helpful.)

____

Move the point about the screen to get the feel of this program.

6. You will want to save this program on a diskette as POINT for use at a later time.

7. Clear the memory and the screen. Exit the graphics mode by typing in the direct mode command **SCREEN 0**. Type in the following program.

```
100 LET S = 0
110 INPUT Y
120 IF Y = 11111 THEN 150
130 LET S = S+Y
140 GOTO 100
150 PRINT S
160 END
```

This program is supposed to add up numbers that are INPUT. The input value that causes the sum to be printed out is 11111. It is not part of the sum.

8. Run the program and each time the INPUT prompt is displayed, type in one number from the following sequence of numbers:

3 1 6 5 11111

What value is printed out for S?

____

Is this value of S the sum of the numbers you INPUT?

____

19. Let's try to find out why. In direct mode type

```
TRON <ENTER>
```

or press function key F7. Now run the program again. What happened?

____

The numbers displayed in brackets on the screen are the line numbers in the order the program executed them. At each input prompt (the ?), enter the same numbers as in Step 18 (be sure to press ENTER after each input). After you have entered 11111, you will notice the last bracketed number is the line number of the END statement. In direct mode type

```
TROFF <ENTER>
```

or press the function key F8. Now run the program again. What happened?

____

TRON Stands for trace on and TROFF stands for trace off.

20. Type in the following line

```
135 PRINT " S= ";S
```

Turn trace on (See Step 18.) List the program. Run the program and INPUT the same values as in Step 18. What are the values of S in line 135 compared to the values INPUT in line 110.

____

Though you may have already discovered the logical error in the program, go through or trace the execution of the program as it appears in the list of bracketed numbers. You can observe that the GOTO statement in line 140 goes to the wrong line, that is, line 100 where S is reset to zero each time).

21. Delete line 135 and EDIT line 140 as follows

```
140 GOTO 110
```

Run the program and INPUT the same values as in Step 18. Is the printout correct this time?

Turn trace off (See Step 18.) Run the program a final time with the same values to verify its correctness.

2. Turn off the computer and go on to the discussion of the objectives.

7–3 DISCUSSION

In this chapter we are concerned mainly with transfer statements, both conditional and unconditional, as well as their use in programs. Before getting to the programming, we will discuss each of the types of transfer statements.

Transfer without Conditions

From the very beginning of the book, we have been using unconditional transfer statements. The following program illustrates the use of the unconditional transfer statement:

```
100 LET Z = 2
110 PRINT Z
120 LET Z = 2*Z
130 GOTO 110
140 END
```

Recall that when ordered to execute a BASIC program, the computer goes to the statement with the lowest line number and then executes the statements in increasing line number order. The only way to interrupt this is with a transfer statement (or, as we will see in the next chapter, a loop command). In the program above, the computer would execute line numbers as follows: 100, 110, 120, 130, 110, 120, 130 110, 120, 130, and so on. The point is that the statement in line 130 causes the computer to jump back to line 110 instead of going to 140. Note that there are no conditions attached to the statement in line 130. This is why the GOTO statement is known as an unconditional transfer statement. It is also clear that the GOTO statement in this case puts the program into a loop and there is no way out. The only way we can get the computer out of the loop is to interrupt the program from the keyboard while it is running.

■ **GOTO is unconditional**

To sum up, if at some point in a program you want the computer to jump to another line without any conditions attached, use the GOTO statement. However, be careful that you don't get the program "hung up" in a loop.

Transfer on Conditions

By now you have most likely established the connection between the IF THEN statements you met in the computer work and the notion of the conditional transfer statement. All conditional transfer statements have the same form. A description of this form and a sample IF THEN statement are given below:

Line # **IF** ⟨relation⟩ ⟨condition⟩ ⟨relation⟩ **THEN** Line #

```
240 IF 3*X - 2 > Y - Z THEN 360
```

No matter what the assertion, all IF THEN statements have this same format. The IF and THEN as well as the two line numbers in the statement require no special explanation. However, the heart of the statement lies in the two expressions separated by the condition that forms the assertion. We must look at them very carefully.

■ **IF THEN statements state conditions.**

In all the examples we have met so far with the exception of the one above, the relations have been either simple variables or constants. This is the type of assertion used in programs most often. Examples might be

```
100 IF U < 3 THEN 250

340 IF S > T THEN 220
```

There are instances, however, in which we might want to use more complicated expressions in the IF THEN statements. In the example following the description of the IF THEN statement, the first relation was

```
3*X-2
```

which is fine providing that X has a value. The second relation,

```
Y-Z
```

can also be used if Y and Z have values. To further illustrate what takes place in a program, suppose that X has the value 1, Y is 10, and Z is 4. The computer will translate the statement

```
240 IF 3*X-2 > Y-Z THEN 360
```

by first substituting the values of X, Y, and Z. This changes the statement to

```
240 IF 1 > 6 THEN 360
```

Sooner or later, all IF THEN statement come down to this form, in which the computer must judge whether an assertion established by two numbers and a condition is true or false. In this case, the assertion 1 > 6 is false. However, an assertion like 4 < 10 would be true. If the assertion is true, the computer will go to the line number following THEN. If the assertion is false, the computer will go to the next higher line number in the program.

■ **IF THEN statements branch if true.**
If false, then next higher line number.

Several conditions may be used in the IF THEN statement. The conditions and their meaning are listed below.

Condition	Meaning
=	Equal to
<	Less than
>	Greater than
<=	Less than or equal to
>=	Greater than or equal to
<>	Not equal to

The IF THEN statement is a branching or transfer statement that depends upon whether an assertion in the statement is true or false. If the condition is true, the computer transfers to the statement following THEN. If the assertion is false, the computer goes to the next higher line number in the program.

The IF THEN ELSE statement is also very useful. It can be used much of the time in place of the IF THEN statement with the added feature that it allows for greater ease in following the flow of the program. In this statement, if the assertion is true, the computer will perform the statement following THEN. If the assertion is false, the computer will perform the statement following ELSE.

In both the IF THEN and IF THEN ELSE statements, when the "statement" following the THEN or the ELSE is a number, the computer will branch to the line with that number. With the use of the conditional transfer statements IF THEN and IF THEN ELSE, the computer can be branched anywhere we desire in a program. This ability, more than anything seen so far, begins to reveal the true power of the computer.

7—4 PROGRAM EXAMPLES

Up to this point our programs have suffered from a serious fault. On one hand, the program might involve repetition but there was no way to stop the process. On the other hand, the program stopped but often tended to be trivial. What we want is a way to have the program accomplish a useful task (which may involve repetition) and then shut itself off. The conditional transfer statements just learned provide a mechanism to do this. Now we will look at several programs that illustrate this capability.

Example 1 - Printout of Number Patterns

Our problem is to write a program that will print out the following number pattern when executed:

```
2  3  4  5   6
7  8  9  10  11
```

There are several characteristics of this pattern which we must think about when writing the program. The first number is 2, and succeeding numbers are spaced across in the standard spacing (five numbers to a line). Each number is 1 greater than the previous one. The last number printed out is 11, then the computer should stop.

Several solutions are possible. A program that is not the most elegant but would still work is

```
100 PRINT 2,3,4,5,6,7,8,9,10,11
110 END
```

You might check this program to see that is does in fact produce the correct number pattern. It also illustrates a very important concept. There is no such thing as the correct program. The only test that can be applied is "Does the program work?" Certainly some programs are cleverer or may accomplish the results more efficiently than others, but this is a separate issue.

Now back to the problem at hand. One way to approach the problem is to make the computer print out the first number in the pattern. We also want to organize the program so that only a single print statement is required. This will require that the program print out the value of a variable that will be changed as the program is executed. We can start our program with the following segment:

```
100 LET X = 2
110 PRINT X,
```

The value of X is set to 2, and this value is printed out in line 110. The comma causes the computer to space across to the next standard printing position. Now we must generate the next value to be printed out. Note that at any point in the number pattern, the next number is just 1 more than the present number. This can be done with

```
120 LET X = X+1
```

Now all that remains is to make a decision about whether to loop back to the print statement or to stop. As long as X is less than or equal to 11, we want to loop back. We can do this with a conditional transfer statement.

```
130 IF X <= 11 THEN 110
```

The program is finished with an END statement.

```
140 END
```

The complete program is

```
100 LET X = 2
110 PRINT X,
120 LET X = X+1
130 IF X <= 11 THEN 110
140 END
```

This program is a simple one and has little practical value other than to illustrate how a conditional transfer statement can get us out of a program at the proper time.

Example 2 - Automobile License Fees

Let's assume than in an attempt to force consumers to use lower-horsepower cars and conserve energy, the state adopts a set of progressive annual license fees based upon the power rating of the car. The criteria and fees are listed below.

Horsepower	License Fee
Up to 50 hp	$0
More than 50 but 100 hp or less	30
More than 100 but 200 hp or less	70
More than 200 but 300 hp or less	150
More than 300 hp	500

We want a program that will produce the following output when executed:

```
INPUT AUTO HP? (You type in horsepower)
LICENSE FEE IS (Computer types out fee)

INPUT AUTO HP? (You type in horsepower)
LICENSE FEE IS (Computer types out fee)
```

(etc.)

Clearly, the only difficult part of the program will be to decide what the fee is. This decision-making process is made to order for the IF THEN statement. To get started we must provide for input of the power rating. We will use P to stand for the power rating of the car. The program can begin with

```
100 PRINT "INPUT AUTO HP ";
110 INPUT P
```

Now, we must work out a method to decide in which license category P lies. A logical way to do this would be to check upward from the low horsepower ratings. First, we can check whether P is 50 or less. If so, then we know the tax is 0.

```
120 IF P <= 50 THEN ________(Fee is 0)
```

The line number following THEN is missing for this reason. If the number in P is less than or equal to 50, we want the computer to jump to a statement that will assign the value 0 to the fee. The problem is that we don't know at this point what line number should be used for this statement. Consequently, we will leave it blank and will return later on and insert the proper value. The note at the right is there to remind us of what the fee is supposed to be if the assertion is true and the branch is taken.

If the assertion in line 120 is false, the computer will go to the next higher line number. In that case we want to check to see if P falls in the next higher category.

```
130 IF P <= 100 THEN ________(Fee is $30)
```

Again, we don't know what line number to use following the THEN but can fill it in later. There are three branch statements left to determine completely which category contains P. Now that the pattern is established, we can include them all at once.

```
140 IF P <= 200 THEN _______(Fee is $70)
150 IF P <= 300 THEN _______(Fee is $150)
160 IF P > 300 THEN _______(Fee is $500)
```

The program to this point is

```
100 PRINT "INPUT AUTO HP ";
110 INPUT P
120 IF P <= 50 THEN _______(Fee is 0)
130 IF P <= 100 THEN _______(Fee is $30)
140 IF P <= 200 THEN _______(Fee is $70)
150 IF P <= 300 THEN _______(Fee is $150)
160 IF P > 300 THEN _______(Fee is $500)
```

Now we can fill in the missing line number in line 120. Since the next line number in the program would be 170, we may as well use it.

```
100 PRINT "INPUT AUTO HP ";
110 INPUT P
120 IF P <= 50 THEN 170
130 IF P <= 110 THEN _______(Fee is $30)
140 IF P <= 200 THEN _______(Fee is $70)
150 IF P <= 300 THEN _______(Fee is $150)
160 IF P > 300 THEN _______(Fee is $500)
170 LET F = 0
180 GOTO _______(PRINT statement)
```

Again, in line 180 we have a missing line number. The reminder is that we want to transfer to a PRINT statement. If the assertion in line 120 is true, the computer jumps to line 170 and assigns the value 0 to F, which stands for the fee. We can go on filling in the missing numbers in lines 130, 140, 150, and 160 using the same pattern. The result is

```
100 PRINT "INPUT AUTO HP ";
110 INPUT P
120 IF P <= 50 THEN 170
130 IF P <= 100 THEN 190
140 IF P <= 200 THEN 210
150 IF P <= 300 THEN 230
160 IF P > 300 THEN 250
170 LET F = 0
180 GOTO ______(PRINT statement)
190 LET F = 30
200 GOTO ______(PRINT statement)
210 LET F = 70
220 GOTO ______(PRINT statement)
230 LET F = 150
240 GOTO ______(PRINT statement)
250 LET F = 500
```

The next line in the program would be 260, which we may as well use for the PRINT statement. The rest of the program follows easily. The complete program is given below.

```
100 PRINT "INPUT AUTO HP ";
110 INPUT P
120 IF P <= 50 THEN 170
130 IF P <= 100 THEN 190
140 IF P <= 200 THEN 210
150 IF P <= 300 THEN 230
160 IF P > 300 THEN 250
170 LET F = 0
180 GOTO 260
190 LET F = 30
200 GOTO 260
210 LET F = 70
220 GOTO 260
230 LET F = 150
240 GOTO 260
250 LET F = 500
260 PRINT "LICENSE FEE IS ";F
270 PRINT
280 GOTO 100
290 END
```

You may have noticed that the conditional transfer statement in line 160 is not necessary. To see why, consider each of the assertions in the IF THEN statements. If the assertion in line 120 is false, we know that P must be greater than 50. Likewise, if each of the following assertions are false, the computer goes to the next higher line number. In particular, suppose the computer reaches line 150 and determines that the assertion is false. This directs the computer to line 160, but then we know that P must be greater than 300 and can therefore print out the fee without any more testing. If we assign the license fee of $500 in line 160, the result is a slightly different program:

```
100 PRINT "INPUT AUTO HP ";
110 INPUT P
120 IF P <= 50 THEN 200
130 IF P <= 100 THEN 220
140 IF P <= 200 THEN 240
150 IF P <= 300 THEN 260
160 LET F = 500
170 PRINT "LICENSE FEE IS ";F
180 PRINT
190 GOTO 100
200 LET F = 0
210 GOTO 170
220 LET F = 30
230 GOTO 170
240 LET F = 70
250 GOTO 170
260 LET F = 150
270 GOTO 170
280 END
```

Both versions of the program will work equally well, and you may have your own version. How you prefer to handle the branches is a matter for you to decide. The only question is whether your program will work.

We have gone through this program in great detail because it often proves difficult for the beginner to write programs involving such search rules. You should study the program until you are convinced that it does accomplish what was desired. Also, try to remember to use the technique of leaving line numbers out when you do not know what they should be, then returning later to fill in the proper values. The comments at the right of the page in these cases will help you remember what you want to happen at that branch point in the program.

Example 3 - Averaging Numbers

Suppose we have numbers in a DATA statement which we wish to average. The problem is that we don't know in advance how many numbers there are. So we will use the strategy of a flag variable to mark the end of the data. The flag will be a number that is very unlikely to occur in the data. We will use the number 9999 for our flag, but you could select one of your own choice if desired.

Here is the way it will work. The DATA statement will always appear as follows:

Line # **DATA** (number),(number),....,(number),9999

The flag 9999 is put in the data after the last number to be averaged. In the program, each time we read a number from the DATA statement we must check to see if it is 9999. If not, we know that the number just read is part of the data to be averaged. If the number is 9999 we know we have read in all the data and can go on to the rest of the program.

An average is computed by dividing the sum of the numbers by the number of numbers. In our program we must compute both these quantities. We will use S to stand for the sum of the numbers and N for the number of numbers. When the program is executed, we do not know what these values will be, so we must set them equal to 0 and then develop their values as we read in numbers from the DATA statements.

The program begins by setting up the initial values of S and N.

```
100 LET S = 0
110 LET N = 0
```

Now we can read a number from the DATA statement and check for the flag value.

```
120 READ X
130 IF X = 9999 THEN _______(Compute average)
```

We are using the method, introduced in the previous example, of leaving a line number blank in the conditional transfer statement until we know what it should be. In this case, if the assertion (X = 9999) is true then we know that all the numbers in the DATA statement have been processed and we are ready to compute the average. If the assertion is false, then the number just read must be part of the data and should be processed. This is done as follows:

```
140 LET S = S+X
150 LET N = N+1
```

In line 140, the value of X (the number just read) is added to the value in S. Remember that the sum of all the numbers to be averaged is being developed in S. In line 150, the number in N is incremented by 1 to record the fact that another number has been processed.

```
160 GOTO 120
```

Now we can fill in the missing number in line 130, since the next line number in the program would normally be 170. In line 170 we compute the average, which we will identify by A. If a typical DATA statement is included, the complete program is

```
100 LET S = 0
110 LET N = 0
120 READ X
130 IF X = 9999 THEN 170
140 LET S = S+X
150 LET N = N+1
160 GOTO 120
170 LET A = S/N
180 PRINT A
190 DATA 4,2,3,6,5,9999
200 END
```

Of course, we can have as many DATA statments as needed to hold the numbers to be averaged. Following the last number in the last DATA statement we put the flag 9999 to mark the end of the data. This gets us out of the READ loop and lets us know when to go on to compute the average. The conditional transfer statement, coupled with the idea of a flag variable, gives us a powerful tool to use in programs.

7–5 FINDING ERRORS IN PROGRAMS

The ability to look at a program and determine whether or not it will accomplish what it is supposed to do is certainly one of the most important skills a beginner can acquire. Probably more to the point, when a program is not doing what it supposed to do, can you find out what is wrong and correct it? These abilities are strange in that, until learned, they appear to be very difficult. However, once learned, the programmer usually has great difficulty understanding why everyone doesn't have the same abilities.

Two separate tasks are involved in troubleshooting programs. First, you need to decide which variables you would like to see additional information about. You can insert PRINT statements into the program to print the values of the variables you are interested in. Second, you need to be able to read the computer display of the trace of the program. These two abilities together will often lead to a quick determination of logical programming errors.

In troubleshooting, the first capability will assist you in finding out where calculations have gone wrong, as we saw in the Discovery Exercises. This will sometimes lead you directly to the logical programming error. However, when it does not, then the use of the tracing capability of the IBM Personal Computer will assist you in finding the error. It is important to remember how to turn tracing on (TRON) and off (TROFF).

7–6 PROBLEMS

You may wish to use TRON (TROFF) to find logical errors in your programs.

1. Write a BASIC program to call for the input of two numbers. Then print out the larger.

2. Write a BASIC program to READ three numbers from a DATA statement and then print out the smallest.

3. Write a program to compute and print out the sum of all the whole numbers between 1 and 100 inclusive.

4. What will happen if the following program is executed? Describe in your own words.

```
100 LET S = 0
110 LET X = 1
120 LET S = S+X
130 LET X = X+2
140 IF X < 100 THEN 120
150 PRINT S
160 END
```

5. In Example 3 in this chapter, edit line 190 as follows:

```
190 DATA 4,2,3,6,5,1111
```

Run the program to detect an error. Use the TRON statement to determine what causes the error. It may be helpful to insert line 155 as follows:

```
155 PRINT "S= ";S;" N= ";N
```

Study the program and write down what will be output if the program is executed. You may wish to run the program to see if you are correct. If the answer is not correct, the tracing techniques covered in this chapter may assist you in arriving at a correct answer.

6. Write a program to find that average of all the positive numbers in a list whose end is marked with the flag 999. The list of numbers is to be typed in at the computer at run time.

7. Suppose you are given a DATA statement that contains a list of numbers of unknown length. However, the end of the list is marked with the flag variable 9999. Write a BASIC program to compute and print out the sum of the numbers in the list between −10 and +10 inclusive.

8. Usually there is a different mark up for supermarkets depending upon the unit cost of the item. Suppose this mark up is based on the following schedule:

Unit Cost	Mark up
0 to $1.00	20%
$1.01 to $2.00	10%
over $2.00	5%

The unit cost is determined by dividing the case price by the number of items in the case. Write a program to compute label price which is unit cost plus mark up. Arrange for prompts and input any way you desire.

. Suppose you agree to work for one cent the first day, two cents the second, four cents the third, eight cents the forth and so on. If there are 22 working days in a month, write a program that will compute your wages (in dollars) for one month.

. Consider the series

```
1 + 1/2 + 1/3 + 1/4 + ...
```

Write a program to find the sum of the first N terms. Use this to find the sum of the first 10, 100, and 1000 terms. Based on these results what do you think the sum would be if we let the series run on forever.

. Study the following program. Can you describe what the program does? You may wish to use the tracing capability of your computer to assist you.

```
100 READ N
110 LET L = 1
120 LET C = 1
130 READ X
140 LET C = C + 1
150 IF X < L THEN 170
160 LET L = X
170 IF C < N THEN 130
180 PRINT L
190 DATA 10
200 DATA 5,83,17,3,47
210 DATA 25,16,41,51,7
220 END
```

Additional information on how the program works may be obtained by inserting line 165 as follows

```
165 PRINT "L IS ";L
```

and running the program.

12. The following program is intended to find the average of N numbers typed in at the terminal. As it stands the program is incorrect. What's wrong?

```
100 PRINT "HOW MANY NUMBERS"
110 INPUT N
120 LET S = 0
130 LET C = 1
140 PRINT "TYPE IN A NUMBER";
150 INPUT X
160 LET S = S + X
170 LET C = C + 1
180 IF C < N THEN 140
190 LET A = S/N
200 PRINT "THE AVERAGE IS"; A
210 END
```

13. The discounted price of an item can be computed by

D = L*(1 - R/100)

where L is the purchase price and R is the discount rate in percent. Write a program that will produce the following output when executed:

```
LIST PRICE ($)?  (You type in price)
DISCOUNT RATE (%)?  (You type in rate)
DISCOUNTED PRICE IS
(Computer types out price) DOLLARS
```

14. There is an interesting sequence of numbers called the Fibonacci numbers. The set begins with 0, 1. Then each succeeding number in the sequence is the sum of the two previous ones. Thus, the Fibonacci sequence is

0, 1, 1, 2, 3, 5, 8,......

Write a BASIC program to compute and print out the first twenty numbers in the Fibonacci sequence.

5. Write a program to accept the input of two numbers. If both the numbers are greater than or equal to 10, print out their sum. If both the numbers are less than 10, print out their product. If one number is greater than or equal to 10 and the other is less than 10, print out the difference between the largest and smallest.

6. An instructor decides to award letter grades on an examination as follows:

90–100	A
80–89	B
60–79	C
50–59	D
0–50	F

Write a program to produce the following output when executed:

INPUT EXAM GRADE ?(You type in numerical grade)
YOUR GRADE IS (Computer types out A, B, C, D, E, or F)

7. If you use 8 percent more electricity each year, in nine years your consumption will double. Thus your doubling time is nine years. It turns out that there is an interesting rule called the "rule of seventy-two" that can be used to compute doubling times. If a quantity grows by R percent in a single period of time, then the number of periods for the quantity to double is given approximately by 72/R. This is the rule of seventy-two. We can compute the growth of a process directly on the computer. In a single growth period, a quantity Q grows according to the relation

$$Q_{new} = Q_{old}(1 + R/100)$$

Thus we can keep track of the growth by repeated use of the relation above. When Q is twice the original value, the corresponding number of growth periods would be the doubling time. Using this approach, write a program that will produce the following output when executed:

GROWTH RATE (%) ? (You type in R)
NUMBER OF GROWTH PERIODS TO DOUBLE IS
(Computer types answer)

Use the program to check out the accuracy of the rule of seventy-two for many different growth rates.

18. A set of integers (whole numbers) is chosen at random from the set 1, 2, 3, 4 and put in a DATA statement. The end of the set is marked with the flag 9999. Write a BASIC program that will compute and print out the number of 1s, 2s, 3s, and 4s in the set. Test your program on the following DATA statement:

```
DATA 3,1,2,1,4,4,1,2,2,2,3,9999
```

19. Write a program that draws short lines (10 units) to the left, right, up or down depending on which of the keys L, R, U, or D is pressed. You should model you program after the program in Step 14 of the Discovery Exercises. Try running the program to see how various lines and figures can be drawn by the program. You may wish to save this program on a diskette as ETCH for later use in Chapter 12.

7–7 PRACTICE TEST

Check your progress with the following practice test. The answers are in the key at the end of the book.

1. What will be output if the following program is executed?

```
100 LET Y = 3
110 LET X = 2*Y
120 PRINT X
130 LET Y = Y+2
140 IF Y <= 10 THEN 110
150 END
```

2. What will be output if the following program is executed?

```
100 READ X
110 DATA 1,2,3
120 IF X < 2 THEN 160
130 IF X = 2 THEN 150
140 PRINT "GOOD"
150 PRINT "BETTER"
160 PRINT "BEST"
170 PRINT
180 GOTO 100
190 END
```

3. Suppose that you decide to buy a number of widgets. The manufacturer is pushing sales so will give reduced prices for quantity purchases. The price detail is as follows:

#Purchased	Price per Widget
20 or less	$2.00
21 to 50	1.80
51 or more	1.50

Write a program that will produce the following output when executed:

```
HOW MANY WIDGETS ?   (You type in purchase quantity)
PRICE PER WIDGET IS (Computer types out unit price)
TOTAL COST OF ORDER IS (Computer types out total)
```

Then keep looping back through the program.

4. Write a program that will print out the number pattern shown below and then stop.

```
0  5  10 15 20 25
30 35 40 45 50 55
etc.
150 155 160 165 170 175
```

5. If you get a ticket for speeding, your fine is based on how much you exceeded the speed limit. Suppose the fine is computed as follows:

Amount over Limit	Fine
1–10 mi/h	$ 5
11–20	10
21–30	20
31–40	40
41 or more	80

Write a BASIC program that will produce the following output when executed:

WHAT WAS SPEED LIMIT ? (You type in)
SPEED ARRESTED AT ? (You type in)
FINE IS (Computer types out fine) **DOLLARS**

CHAPTER 8

LOOPING AND FUNCTIONS

8—1 OBJECTIVES

In this chapter we will learn about two interesting characteristics of BASIC which will provide new and powerful programming capability. The objectives are as follows.

Built-in Looping

We have already learned how to loop programs using either the unconditional or conditional transfer statements. BASIC has special statements to take care of looping automatically. These statements simplify the programming task and provide flexibility in programs.

Built-in Functions

BASIC contains a number of built-in functions that can be called on to perform specific tasks. We will look at some of the simpler of these functions that involve numerical computations and see how they can be used to advantage.

Program Applications

We will continue with activities designed to draw you into programming. Remember that the overall objective of the book is to teach you how to write BASIC language programs.

8–2 DISCOVERY EXERCISES

Computer Work

1. Turn on the computer, bring up BASICA and enter the following program:

```
100 LET Y = 10
110 PRINT Y,
120 LET Y = Y+5
130 IF Y <= 50 THEN 110
140 END
```

Study the program and then execute it. Record what happened.

____

Which statement in the program determines the difference in the numbers that were typed out?

____

2. Clear out the program in memory. Now enter the following program:

```
100 FOR Y = 10 TO 50 STEP 5
110 PRINT Y,
120 NEXT Y
130 END
```

Execute the program and record what happened.

____

Compare the output to that obtained from the program in Step 1.

3. Since the two programs just executed produce the same output, it is reasonable to assume that the statements must be related in some way. Type

```
100 FOR Y = 10 TO 50 STEP 10
```

Display the program in memory and study it. What do you think will happen if we execute this program?

____

See if you were right. Execute the program and record the results below.

4. Now let's try a few different ideas out on the program. Type

```
100 FOR Y = 0 TO 5 STEP 1
```

Display the program. What do you think this program will do?

Execute the program and write down the output below.

Now type

```
100 FOR Y = 0 TO 5
```

Display the program. What do you think this program will do?

Execute the program and record what happened.

Now compare line 100 in the program just executed with line 100 in the program in Step 4. If the difference between the numbers to be printed out is 1, is the STEP part of the statement necessary?

Let's try a different tactic. Type

```
100 FOR Y = 20 TO 10 STEP -2
```

Display the program and study it. What do you think this program will do?

Execute the program and record the output.

____

7. All right, now type

```
100 FOR Y = 10 TO 20 STEP -2
```

Display the program. What do you think will happen now if we execute the program?

____

Execute the program and write down what happened.

____

What we have done here is to lead you into a potential trap in BASIC. What seems to be the problem?

____

8. So far the step sizes in the FOR NEXT statements have worked out without any problem. Let's try a new step size that might not come out even when compared to the limits in the FOR NEXT statement. Type

```
100 FOR Y = 2 TO 9 STEP 3
```

Display the program. Write down what you think will be printed out?

____

Execute the program and record what happened.

____

9. We will go on now to some more involved situations involving FOR NEXT statements. Clear out the program in memory and enter the following program:

```
100 FOR X = 1 TO 3
110 FOR Y = 1 TO 4
120 PRINT X,Y
130 NEXT Y
140 NEXT X
150 END
```

Execute the program and record the output.

____

0. Now type

```
100 FOR X = 1 TO 2
```

Execute this new program and record the output.

____

Compare the two number patterns you have just obtained. Can you see the connection between the patterns and the limits in the FOR NEXT statements?

____

1. Let's modify the program a bit more. Type

```
100 FOR X = 1 TO 3
110 FOR Y = 1 TO 2
```

Display this program and study it. What do you think will be output if it is executed?

____

Try it and see if you were right.

____

12. One more time. Type

```
100 FOR X = 1 TO 2
110 FOR Y = 1 TO 2
```

Display the program and write down what you think will be typed out when the program is executed.

____

Execute the program and record the results below.

____

On the listing of the program just executed, draw a line from the line number of the FOR X statement to the line number of the NEXT X statement. Do the same thing for the FOR Y and the NEXT Y statements. Do these lines cross?

____

13. Now type

```
100 FOR Y = 1 TO 2
110 FOR X = 1 TO 2
```

Display the program. What do you think will be output by this program?

____

Execute the program and record what happened.

____

On the listing of this program, connect the FOR X and the NEXT X line numbers with a line just as you did in Step 12. Do the same thing for the FOR Y and the NEXT Y statements. Do these lines cross? Compare with the same situation in Step 12.

____

Does this suggest a way to avoid getting into trouble using more than one FOR NEXT combination in a single program?

4. In Chapter 6 we experimented with the TAB function to get variable spacing in the output. Now that we have the FOR NEXT statements at our disposal, let's go back to the TAB function. Clear out the program in memory and enter the following program:

```
100 FOR X = 1 TO 5
110 PRINT TAB(X);
120 FOR Y = X TO 5
130 PRINT "Y";
140 NEXT Y
150 PRINT
160 NEXT X
170 END
```

Take a few moments to study the program. What output do you think the program will produce?

See if you were right. Execute the program and record the output below.

5. Clear out the program in memory. Enter the program below.

```
10 FOR J = 1 TO 2
20 READ L$
30 DATA L8,L16
40 FOR I = 1 TO 4
50 LET P$ = "O = I; CDEFGAB"
60 PLAY L$ + P$
70 NEXT I
80 PLAY "O5C"
90 NEXT J
100 END
```

Study the program. Note the 0 rather than Ø in lines 50 and 80. How many octaves are played when the notes have length 8 (eighth notes)?

____

Run the program. Were you right?

____

Is line 80 executed 2, 4 or 8 times?

____

16. Clear out the program in memory. Enter the program below.

```
100 INPUT A
110 LET B = SQR(A)
120 PRINT B
130 GOTO 100
140 END
```

Execute the program and at the INPUT prompt, type 4. What happened?

____

Now type in 9 and record the results.

____

One more time. Type in 25. What happened?

____

Finally, type in 10. What happened?

____

All right, what happens to A in the expression SQR(A) in line 110 of the program? In other words, what does SQR do?

____

7. Jump the computer out of the input loop. Type

```
110 LET B = INT(A)
```

Execute the program for the following values of A. In each case, record the output of the program.

A	Output
1	______
3.4	______
256.78	______
0	______
-1	______
-2.3	______

Examine the output you have recorded above and compare each number with the corresponding value of A that you typed in. What does the INT(A) function do?

____

If you had trouble understanding what was happening to the negative values of A, don't worry at this point. We will review this completely later.

8. Jump the computer out of the input loop. Type

```
110 LET B = SGN(A)
```

Display the program and review the program structure to refresh your memory about how the program works. Execute the program for each of the following values of A. In each case, record the output.

A	Output
1.5	______
43	______
128.3	______
0	______
-1	______
-1.2	______
-345.7	______
4.7	______
-5.8	______

Examine the output above carefully. What does the SGN function do?

____

19. One more function. Jump the computer out of the input loop. Type

```
110 LET B = ABS(A)
```

Execute the program for each of the values of A given below. Again, record the output in each case.

A	Output
3.4	______
0	______
-3.4	______
-2	______
-8.45	______
8.45	______

Examine the output. What does the ABS function do?

---

0. This concludes the computer work for now. Jump the computer out of the input loop and turn off the computer.

8–3 DISCUSSION

The techniques explored in the computer work can bring new power to the programs we write. We need to understand exactly how these new tools can be used to best advantage.

Built-in Looping

In the previous chapters we learned how to loop programs under the control of transfer statements. The unconditional (GO TO) statement was useful but could sometimes result in a loop with no way out. The conditional (IF THEN) and (IF THEN ELSE) statements provided a way to loop the program as desired and also a way to get out of the loop. All of these are good techniques. However, BASIC has a very elegant way to take care of looping which takes a large burden from the back of the programmer. We will now go over this new method, which uses the FOR NEXT statements.

All FOR statements have the same format. This format and a typical statement are shown below.

Line# **FOR**⟨variable⟩ = ⟨relation⟩**TO**⟨relation⟩ **STEP**⟨relation⟩

```
120 FOR X = 1 TO 9 STEP 2
```

The things that can change in FOR statements are the variable and the three relations. If the STEP is left out of the statement, the computer will use a step size of 1. We can write many different forms of the FOR statement. A few are given below to illustrate the range of possibilities.

```
130 FOR J = 2 TO 8
130 FOR T = 25 TO 10 STEP -2
130 FOR W = -20 TO 10 STEP 2
130 FOR X = 3*Z TO A*B STEP D
```

In general, we can write any legal BASIC statement in the relations involved in the FOR statement provided, of course, that the variables used have been properly defined in the program.

■ Use FOR NEXT statements for looping.

The FOR statement opens a loop. We close the loop with the NEXT statement. How this is done is illustrated in the following example:

```
200 FOR X = 2 TO 18 STEP 2 (Opens loop)
.
.
.
Program lines inside loop
.
.
.
340 NEXT X (Closes loop)
```

In the NEXT statement, the variable must be the same as that in the FOR statement that opened the loop.

It is important to completely understand how these loops work. In the example above, when the program reaches line 200 the first time, X is set equal to 2. Then the computer works through the lines until line 340 is reached. This closes the loop and directs the computer back to line 200 and the next value of X, which in this case would be 4. The computer stays in the loop until the value of X exceeds the limit of 18. Then, instead of going through the statements inside the loop, the computer jumps to the line number following the NEXT statement used to close the loop. Let's look at an example to see the FOR NEXT statements in action once more.

```
100 LET A = 1
110 FOR X = 1 TO 6 STEP 2
120 LET A = 2*A
130 PRINT A, X
140 NEXT X
150 END
```

Since only two variables are involved in this program (A and X), we will list the line numbers in the order the computer encounters them and the corresponding values of the variables.

Line Number	A	X
100	1	
110	1	1
120	2	1
130	2	1
140	2	1
110	2	3
120	4	3
130	4	3
140	4	3
110	4	5
120	8	5
130	8	5
140	8	5
110	8	7*
150	**	

* Jumps out of loop
** Program stops

Study the sequence of line numbers and the corresponding values of A and X until you are certain that you understand how the FOR NEXT statements control the loop.

Quite often, more complicated loop structures are required in a program. The structure can be as involved as desired provided that the loops do not cross. The example below illustrates a segment of a program with crossed loops.

```
100 FOR A = 2 TO 20
110 FOR B = 4 TO 8

   Loops cross!

240 NEXT A
250 NEXT B
```

Another example with crossed loops is

```
100 FOR I = 0 TO 20 STEP 2
110 FOR A = 10 TO 2 STEP -1
120 FOR B = 1 TO 4

   Outer loop OK; inner loops cross!

170 NEXT A
180 NEXT B
190 NEXT I
```

The following example illustrates a complicated loop structure in which the loops are organized correctly:

```
100 FOR X = 1 TO 10
110 FOR Y = 2 TO 4
.
.
140 NEXT Y
.
.
170 FOR Z = 1 TO 5
.
.
210 FOR K = 20 TO 10 STEP -2
.
.
270 NEXT K
.
.
310 NEXT Z
.
.
410 NEXT X
```

In this example we have double loops and loops within loops. Remember, though, that any combination may be used in a program provided that lines connecting the FOR statements and their corresponding NEXT statements do not cross. If they do, the computer will signal an error and stop.

■ **Don't cross your FOR NEXT loops!**

Built-in Functions

One of the advantages of a modern digital computer is that sets of instructions can be preprogrammed to accomplish any desired task. Since there are many computing tasks that are routinely needed, IBM has preprogrammed some of these in the form of functions. With these built-in functions in BASIC, the programmer can perform very complicated mathematical operations without difficulty. We will look at several of these functions and see exactly how they work.

Function	Action
SQR(X)	Square root of X
INT(X)	Integer part of X
SGN(X)	Sign of X
ABS(X)	Absolute value of X

Let's use the first function, SQR(X), to see how all the functions operate in general. First, X is called the argument of the function. If this definition bothers you, then think of X as "what the functions works on". If we use SQR(X) in a program, we are instructing the computer to look up the value of X, then take the square root of the number. For example,

SQR(36) = 6

SQR(64) = 8

SQR(81) = 9

SQR(2) = 1.414214

and so on. The only limitation is that we can't take the square root of a negative number. If the computer tried to evaluate SQR(–6), for example, it would signal an error and stop.

The argument of the function can be as complicated as needed in the program. If the computer runs across an expression like

SQR(X+4*Y)

it will look up the values of X and Y, carry out the calculation indicated, then take the square root. This characteristic is true for all the functions.

INT(X) takes the integer part of X. The term integer is just a high-class way to say "whole number." Thus, 2 is an integer while 23.472 is not. If we take the integer part of a number, we simple forget about everything following the decimal point. Thus

INT(3.1593) = 3

INT(54.76) = 54

INT(0.362) = 0

However, negative numbers require special attention. What is really happening when we take the integer part of a number is that we go to the first integer less than or equal to the number. Using this rule we see that

INT(–2) = –2

INT(–.93) = –1

and so on. Note carefully that the INT function does not round off a number. Often beginners are somewhat confused about this.

■ **The integer part of a number is the first integer less than the number.**

SGN(X) is a very interesting function. If X (the function argument) is positive, SGN(X) is +1. If X is negative, SGN(X) is –1.

If X is 0, SGN(X) is 0. In effect, SGN(X) returns the sign of X, either +1, −1, or 0. Therefore,

SGN(4.568) = +1

SGN(375) = +1

SGN(0) = 0

SGN(−5.93) = −1

SGN(−4) = −1

At this point it may not be clear to you why such a function could be useful. It turns out that the SGN function is very useful, however, and has many applications. For the time being, we will be content just to learn how the function works. ABS(X) simply tells the computer to ignore the sign of X. In effect, it converts all values of X, other than 0, to positive numbers. So

ABS(4.5) = 4.5

ABS(−4.5) = 4.5

ABS(95.34) = 95.34

ABS(−95.34) = 95.34

ABS(0) = 0

There are many other built-in functions in BASIC. However, most of these involve more mathematical knowledge than we can assume in this book. If you have had the mathematics necessary to understand what the functions are doing, you will have no difficulty learning how to use them. If you are interested, consult the *BASIC* reference manual. We will take up some functions that involve strings of characters in Chapter 10.

The built-in functions we have been discussing are used in BASIC statements. Examples of lines that utilize such functions might be

```
100 LET X = SQR(Y)
100 LET Z = 3*INT(C)+ABS(D)
```

The built in functions can be used within functions as

```
100 LET Y = INT(SQR(X)+3*ABS(Z))
```

■ **Any BASIC expression can be the argument of BASIC functions.**

8–4 PROGRAM EXAMPLES

The example programs that we will study have been chosen to show you how we can use automatic looping and the built-in functions to make programming easier.

Example 1 - Finding the Average of a Group of Numbers

In the previous chapter, we used the problem of finding an average for one of the example programs. Let's return to the same problem but use a different method. We want the program to produce the following printout when executed:

```
HOW MANY NUMBERS (You type in)
ENTER THE NUMBERS, ONE AT A TIME
? (You type in the numbers)
THE AVERAGE IS (Computer types out average)
```

The first few lines should be easy for you to write by now.

```
100 PRINT "HOW MANY NUMBERS";
110 INPUT N
120 PRINT "ENTER THE NUMBERS, ONE AT A TIME"
```

Now we must arrange for the input of N numbers but must also keep in mind that we are supposed to compute the average of the numbers. So initially we will set S (which will be used to sum the numbers) equal to 0.

```
130 LET S = 0
```

The input of N numbers and the summing up of them is an ideal task for the FOR NEXT statements.

```
140 FOR I = 1 TO N
150 INPUT X
160 LET S = S+X
170 NEXT I
```

Notice that we don't use I, the loop variable, except to count the numbers as they are input. When all the numbers are in, the computer will jump out of the loop to the next higher line number after 170. When this happens, S will contain the sum of all the values of X that were typed in. Since we know that N is the number of numbers typed in, we can immediately compute the average.

```
180 LET A = S/N
```

The rest of the program follows without difficulty.

```
190 PRINT "THE AVERAGE IS";A
200 END
```

The complete program is

```
100 PRINT "HOW MANY NUMBERS";
110 INPUT N
120 PRINT "ENTER THE NUMBERS, ONE AT A TIME"
130 LET S = 0
140 FOR I = 1 TO N
150 INPUT X
160 LET S = S+X
170 NEXT I
180 LET A = S/N
190 PRINT "THE AVERAGE IS";A
200 END
```

Example 2 - Temperature Conversion Table

In one of the earlier programs we used the relation

$$C = 5/9*(F-32)$$

to convert from degrees Fahrenheit to degrees Celsius. Now let's generate a conversion table as follows:

Degrees F	Degrees C
0	–17.77777
5	–15
10	–12.22222
etc.	
100	37.77777

First we should print out the heading and the space before the table itself begins.

```
100 PRINT "DEGREES F","DEGREES C"
110 PRINT
```

We can use a FOR NEXT loop to generate the values of F, which can then be converted to C and printed out.

```
120 FOR F = 0 TO 100 STEP 5
130 LET C = 5*(F-32)/9
140 PRINT F,C
150 NEXT F
```

Finally we need the END statement.

```
160 END
```

The whole program is given below.

```
100 PRINT "DEGREES F","DEGREES C"
110 PRINT
120 FOR F = 0 TO 100 STEP 5
130 LET C = 5*(F-32)/9
140 PRINT F,C
150 NEXT F
160 END
```

Example 3 - Exact Division

We now want to write a program that will compute all the integers (whole numbers) that divide exactly into another integer. To illustrate, suppose we take 8 as the test integer. The problem is to find all the integers that will divide exactly into 8 with no remainder. The rule to use is

If N/X = INT(N/X) then there is no remainder
If N/X ⟨⟩ INT(N/X) then there is a remainder

Now let's write a program to produce the following output when executed:

INPUT A POSITIVE WHOLE NUMBER? (You type in)
THE NUMBERS WHICH DIVIDE EXACTLY ARE
(Computer types out first number, computer types out second number, etc.)

The program begins easily.

```
100 PRINT "INPUT A POSITIVE WHOLE NUMBER";
110 INPUT N
120 PRINT "THE NUMBERS WHICH DIVIDE EXACTLY ARE"
```

Now we have to look at each of the whole numbers between 1 and N. Of course, this is ideal for the FOR NEXT loops. Using the rule given above, we can see whether or not each number divides exactly.

```
130 FOR X = 1 TO N
140 IF N/X <> INT(N/X) THEN 160
150 PRINT X,
160 NEXT X
```

Finally we need the END statement.

```
170 END
```

The complete program is

```
100 PRINT "INPUT A POSITIVE WHOLE NUMBER";
110 INPUT N
120 PRINT "THE NUMBERS WHICH DIVIDE EXACTLY ARE"
130 FOR X = 1 TO N
140 IF N/X <> INT(N/X) THEN 160
150 PRINT X,
160 NEXT X
170 END
```

You might try the program out using fairly large values of N. How could you make the program run in half the time?

Example 4 - Depreciation Schedule

When a company invests in equipment, the investment is depreciated over a number of years for tax purposes. This means that the value of the equipment is decreased each year (due to use, wear, and tear), and the amount of decrease is a tax-deductible item. One of the methods used to compute depreciation is the "sum-of-the-years'-digits" schedule. To illustrate, suppose a piece of equipment has a lifetime of 5 years. The sum of the years' digits would be

$$1 + 2 + 3 + 4 + 5 = 15$$

The depreciation the first year will be 5/15 of the initial value. The depreciation fraction the second year will be 4/15, and so on. If the equipment had an initial value of $3000, the depreciation schedule would be

End of Year	Depreciation Fraction	Depreciation	Current Value
1	5/15	1000	2000
2	4/15	800	1200
3	3/15	600	600
4	2/15	400	200
5	1/15	200	0

Our problem is to write a BASIC program to generate depreciation schedules by the "sum-of-the-years'-digits" method. The output should be as follows:

```
WHAT IS THE INITIAL ASSET VALUE? (You type in)
WHAT IS THE ASSET LIFE IN YEARS? (You type in)

END OF    DEPRECIATION    DEPRECIATION    CURRENT
 YEAR       FRACTION                    ASSET VALUE
(Computer prints out table)
```

The first few lines of the program can be written without any explanation:

```
100 PRINT "WHAT IS THE INITIAL ASSET VALUE";
110 INPUT P
120 PRINT "WHAT IS THE ASSET LIFE IN YEARS";
130 INPUT N
140 PRINT
150 PRINT "END OF","DEPRECIATION","DEPRECIATION",
    "CURRENT"
160 PRINT " YEAR","FRACTION"," ","ASSET VALUE"
170 PRINT
```

Next we must compute the sum-of-the-years' digits.

```
180 LET S = 0
190 FOR I = 1 TO N
200 LET S = S+I
210 NEXT I
```

Now we compute the schedule and print it out. We will use the variable P1 to keep track of the current asset value.

```
220 LET P1 = P
230 FOR I = 1 TO N
240 LET F = (N+1-I)/S
250 LET D = P*F
260 LET P1 = P1-D
270 PRINT I,F,D,P1
280 NEXT I
```

In line 240, F is the depreciation fraction for the Ith year. You can check this out for various values of I to ensure that the expression does generate the correct value of F. In line 250, D is the depreciation. The only thing missing now is the END statement.

```
290 END
```

The complete program is

```
100 PRINT "WHAT IS THE INITIAL ASSET VALUE";
110 INPUT P
120 PRINT "WHAT IS THE ASSET LIFE IN YEARS";
130 INPUT N
140 PRINT
150 PRINT "END OF","DEPRECIATION","DEPRECIATION",
    "CURRENT"
160 PRINT " YEAR","FRACTION"," ","ASSET VALUE"
170 PRINT
180 LET S = 0
190 FOR I = 1 TO N
200 LET S = S+I
210 NEXT I
220 LET P1 = P
230 FOR I = 1 TO N
240 LET F = (N+1-I)/S
250 LET D = P*F
260 LET P1 = P1-D
270 PRINT I,F,D,P1
280 NEXT I
290 END
```

Try out the program for different inputs. Of course, you can use this to set up schedules to be used on your tax returns. Impress the Internal Revenue Service with your computer-generated depreciation schedules!

8–5 PROBLEMS

1. Write a program to generate a table of numbers and their square roots. The table should look as follows:

```
N          SQR(N)
2.0        1.414214
2.1        1.449138
2.2        1.483240

etc.

3.9        1.974842
4.0        2.000000
```

2. Write a program to count from 0 to 500 by tens and print out the results.

3. Write a program to accept the input of a number N, then print out the even numbers greater than 0 but less than or equal to N.

4. Write a program to print out a conversion table from inches to centimeters. There are 2.54 centimeters in one inch. Include the appropriate headings. Start the table at 0 and continue to 10 inches in steps of 0.5 inch.

5. What will be printed out if the following program is run?

```
100 FOR X = 10 TO 1 STEP - 1
110 PRINT TAB(X); "ABCDEFGHIJ"
120 NEXT X
130 END
```

6. Study the following program. What will be output if it is executed?

```
100 FOR I = 1 TO 5
110 READ A
120 LET B = INT(A)-SGN(A)*2
130 PRINT B
140 NEXT I
150 DATA 2,2,-3,10,0,-1.5
160 END
```

7. What will be printed out if we execute the following program?

```
100 FOR X = 1 TO 10
120 LET Y = 2*X
130 FOR Z = 1 TO 5
140 LET U = Z + Y
150 FOR V = 1 TO 3
160 PRINT V + U
170 NEXT Z
180 NEXT V
190 NEXT X
200 END
```

8. The following program won't work. What's wrong?

```
100 FOR X = -10 TO +10 STEP 2
110 PRINT X, SQR(X)
120 NEXT X
130 END
```

9. Explain what the following program does:

```
100 FOR X = 1 TO 5
110 READ Y
120 LET Z = INT(100*Y+.5)/100
130 PRINT Z
140 NEXT X
150 DATA 1.06142,27.5292,138.021
160 DATA .423715,51.9132
170 END
```

10. Write a program to print out the following pattern of asterisks:

```
* * * * * * *
  * * * * *
    * * *
      *
```

No fair using more than two PRINT statements!

The following are the PLAY sublanguage statements for the song Frere Jacque.

```
PLAY "C4D4E4C4 P8 C4D4E4C4 P8 E4F4G4 P4 E4F4G4 P4"
PLAY "G8A8G8F8 P32 E8C2 P4 G8A8G8F8 P32 E8C2"
PLAY "P4 C4 O3G4 O4C4 P6 C4 O3G4 O4C4"
```

Use these statements to write a program that plays these notes at four different tempos. The tempo may be set with the PLAY statement

```
PLAY "T = I;"
```

When I is 1, the notes will be played as whole notes.

N! is read "N factorial" and means the product of all the counting numbers from 1 to N inclusive. For example

$$3! = (1)(2)(3) = 6$$
$$5! = (1)(2)(3)(4)(5) = 120$$

and so on. Write a program to call for the input of N. Then compute and print out N! If you try out this program on the computer, you may be surprised to find that there are values of N less than 100 that produce factorials too large for the computer to handle. The factorial of N is an extremely rapidly increasing function.

Write a BASIC program to call for N grades to be input. Compute and print out (1) the highest grade, (2) the lowest grade, and (3) the average of the grades.

What, if anything, is wrong with the following program?

```
100 FOR X = 1 TO 2
110 FOR Y = 2 TO 6
120 PRINT X+Y
130 NEXT Y
140 FOR Z = 1 TO 3
150 PRINT X+Z
160 NEXT X
170 NEXT Z
180 END
```

15. What will be output if the following program is executed?

```
100 FOR X = 1 TO 4
110 FOR Y = 1 TO 3
120 LET Z = X*Y
130 PRINT Z,
140 NEXT Y
150 PRINT
160 NEXT X
170 END
```

16. Suppose you decide to invest $1000 on the first of each year for 10 years at an annual interest rate of 6 percent. At the end of the tenth year, the value of the investment will be $13,971.64. To see how this could be computed, use the following formula:

$$\$NEW = (\$OLD + I)(1 + R/100).$$

In this formula, R is the annual interest rate in percentage. I is the annual investment, $OLD is the value of the investment at the beginning of each year, and $NEW is the value of the investment at the end of the year. Thus, $NEW becomes $OLD for the next year. Write a BASIC program which will produce the following output when executed:

WHAT IS THE ANNUAL INVESTMENT? (You type in)
WHAT IS THE ANNUAL INTEREST RATE (%)? (You type)
HOW MANY YEARS? (You type in)
AT THE END OF THE LAST YEAR THE VALUE OF THE INVESTMENT WILL BE (Computer types answer)

17. The DATA statements below contain the time worked by a number of employees during a 1-week period.

```
190 DATA 5
200 DATA 2, 4.8, 8, 10, 8, 7, 10
201 DATA 5, 3.75, 7, 8, 8, 6, 10
202 DATA 1, 3.25, 8, 10, 6, 8, 8
203 DATA 4, 5, 8, 10, 6, 10, 6
204 DATA 3, 4.25, 6, 6, 8, 10, 7
```

The number in line 190 gives the number of employees to follow. Each of the DATA lines after line 190 contains a weekly record for one employee. The data are an employee number, the hourly rate, and the hours worked Monday through Friday. The employee receives time and a half for everything over 40 hours per week. Write a BASIC program using these DATA statements to compute and print out the employee number and the gross pay for the week for each of the employees.

3. Assume that the following DATA statements give the performance of the students in an English class on three examinations:

```
190 DATA 6
200 DATA 3, 90, 85, 92
201 DATA 1, 75, 80, 71
202 DATA 6, 100, 82, 81
203 DATA 5, 40, 55, 43
204 DATA 2, 60, 71, 68
205 DATA 4, 38, 47, 42
```

The number in line 190 is the number of students in the class. Each of the DATA statements that follow gives the performance for a single student. The information is the student ID number, grade 1, grade 2, and grade 3. Thus, as shown in line 202, student 6 got examination grades of 100, 82, and 81. Write a program using these DATA statements to compute and print out each student's ID number and his or her course grade. Assume that the first two examination grades are weighted 25 percent each toward the overall grade and the last grade is weighted 50 percent.

8–6 PRACTICE TEST

See how well you have learned the material in the chapter by taking this practice test. The answers are given at the end of the book.

. What will be printed if the following program is executed?

```
100 FOR Y = 20 TO 1 STEP -2
110 PRINT Y,
120 NEXT Y
130 END
```

2. What will be printed out if the following program is executed?

```
100 FOR A = 1 TO 4
110 FOR B = 1 TO 3
120 PRINT A*B,
130 NEXT B
140 NEXT A
150 END
```

3. Fill in the blanks.

a. SQR(36) = ______
b. INT(7.13) = ______
c. ABS(–22.8) = ______
d. SGN(–1.3) = ______

4. What (if anything) is wrong with the following program?

```
100 FOR I = 1 TO 5
110 FOR J = 2 TO 5
120 PRINT I, J
130 NEXT I
140 NEXT J
150 END
```

5. Miles can be converted to kilometers by multiplying the number of miles by 1.609. Write a program to produce the following output when executed.

```
Miles       Kilometers
-----       ----------
10          16.09
15          24.135
20          32.18

etc.

100          160.9
```

. Numerical information is loaded into DATA statements as follows:

```
100 DATA 10
110 DATA 25, 21, 24, 21, 26, 27, 25, 24, 23, 24
```

The number in line 100 gives the number of numbers to be processed in the rest of the DATA statements. Write a program using these statements to compute the average of the numbers excluding the one in line 100.

. The PLAY statement

```
PLAY "T100;"
```

will set the tempo of the music so that 100 quarter notes will be played each minute. At how many tempos will the following program PLAY *Row, Row, Row Your Boat.*

```
100 FOR I = 95 TO 255 STEP 32
110 PLAY "T = I;"
120 PLAY "O2C4C4C8 P32 D12 P32 E8 P8"
130 PLAY "E8 P32 D8E8 P32 F8"
140 PLAY "G8 P4 O3C12C12C12 O2G12G12G12E12"
150 PLAY "E12E12C4 P12 G8 P16 F8E8 P16 D8C8 P4"
160 NEXT I
170 END
```

CHAPTER 9

WORKING WITH COLLECTIONS OF NUMBERS

9–1 OBJECTIVES

In this chapter we will apply some of the ideas learned earlier to collections of numbers. New concepts will be introduced which will expand the capability of BASIC. The objectives are as follows.

Single– and Double–Subscripted Varibles

Much more powerful programs can be written using subscripted variables. Therefore we will see what subscripted variables are and how to use them.

Program Applications

We will study BASIC programs that take advantage of the power of subscripted variables.

9–2 DISCOVERY EXERCISES

Since students tend to have difficulty with this material, some introduction is needed before the computer work is started.

Subscripts

When working with groups of numbers we must be able to distinguish members of the group from one another. This is the reason for subscripts. Before getting into subscripts, however, we need to add two important words to our computer vocabulary. We could use the word collection to describe a group of numbers, but it turns out that two other words are more commonly used. The words are matrix and array. For our purposes they both mean the same thing: a "collection of numbers." If you had seen the terms matrix and array before understanding a little about what the words mean you might have gotten unnecessarily excited. Remember, then, the terms matrix and array mean a collection of numbers.

To see how this works, let's look at the array given below.

$$Y_1 = 9$$

$$Y_2 = 10$$

$$Y_3 = 7$$

$$Y_4 = 14$$

$$Y_5 = 12$$

$$Y_6 = 15$$

The name of the array is Y. Its size is six, since there are six elements (or numbers) in it. The numbers 9, 10, 7, 14, 12, and 15 are the elements in the array. The numbers printed to the right and slightly below the Ys are called subscripts. Each subscript merely points to one element in the array. Thus, Y(4) means the fourth number in the array, which in this case is 14. We read Y(4) as "Y sub four." The third number in the array would be called "Y sub three," and so on. This array is one-dimensional, since it takes only a single number (or subscript) to locate a given element in the array.

Now let's look at a more complicated example but one which still uses the ideas introduced above.

$$Z_{1,1} = 4 \quad Z_{1,2} = 9 \quad Z_{1,3} = 5$$

$$Z_{2,1} = 3 \quad Z_{2,2} = 8 \quad Z_{2,3} = 7$$

In this example there are six elements in the array Z. However, this is a two-dimensional array, since we must specify which row and column we want. The first subscript gives the row number; the second specifies the column. Z(2,1) is read as "Z sub two one" and means the element of Z at the second row and first column. Likewise, the element at row 1, column 3 would be identified as Z(1,3) and would be read "Z sub one three."

To sum up, we will work with two kinds of matrices or arrays. The one-dimensional array needs only a single number to locate an element in that array. The two-dimensional array needs two numbers (a row number and a column number) to locate an element. The one-dimensional array is also associated with the idea of a single-subscripted variable. Likewise, the double-subscripted variable is used in the two-dimensional array. With this brief introduction, you are ready for the computer work.

■ **MATRIX and ARRAY mean <u>collections</u> of numbers.**

Computer Work

1. Turn on the computer, bring up BASICA and enter the following program:

```
100 LET X(1) = 21
110 LET X(2) = 13
120 LET X(3) = 16
130 LET X(4) = 8
140 LET X(5) = 11
150 PRINT X(1)
160 END
```

What do you think will be printed out if we execute the program?

Execute the program and record what happened.

2. Now modify the program to print out the fourth value of X. Execute the program. Did it work?

3. All right, type

```
150 PRINT X(3) + X(4)
```

Display the program and study it briefly. What do you think will happen if we execute the program?

____

Execute the program and see if you were right. Record below what actually was printed out.

____

4. Type

```
150 FOR I = 1 TO 5
152 PRINT X(I)
154 NEXT I
```

Display the program. What do you think will be printed out by this program?

____

See if you were right. Record below what happened when you executed the program.

____

5. Modify this program to print out only the first three values of the array X. Record below what happened when you tried this.

____

6. Again modify the program, but this time so that the first value of the array, then every other one, will be printed out. Record what happened below.

____

7. Clear out the program in memory. Enter the following program:

```
100 LET Y(1,1) = 2
110 LET Y(1,2) = 5
120 LET Y(1,3) = 1
130 LET Y(2,1) = 2
140 LET Y(2,2) = 4
150 LET Y(2,3) = 3
160 PRINT Y(1,3)
170 END
```

Display the program and make sure you have entered it correctly. What do you think this program does?

____

Execute the program and record what was printed out.

____

8. Type

```
160 PRINT Y(2,2) + Y(1,3) + Y(1,1)
```

Display the program. What will this program do if executed?

____

Execute the program and see if you were right.

9. Type

```
160 LET S = 0
162 FOR J = 1 TO 3
164 LET S = S+Y(1,J)
166 NEXT J
168 PRINT S
```

Display the program and study it carefully. What will happen if we execute this program?

____

Execute the program and record what was printed out.

____

Explain in your own words what is taking place in the program.

____

10. Type

```
162 FOR I = 1 TO 2
164 LET S = S+Y(I,2)
166 NEXT I
```

Display the program. What is the program doing now?

____

Execute the program and write down what was printed out.

____

Again try to explain in your own words what is happening.

____

11. Now type

```
162 FOR I = 1 TO 2
164 FOR J = 1 TO 3
166 LET S = S+Y(I,J)
168 NEXT J
170 NEXT I
172 PRINT S
180 END
```

Display the program and think a minute about it. In particular, compare what you see now to what was going on in Steps 9 and 10. What does this program do?

____

Execute the program and record what was typed out.

2. Clear out the program in memory. Type in the following program:

```
100 DIM X(12), Y(12)
110 FOR I = 1 TO 12
120 READ X(I), Y(I)
130 NEXT I
140 PRINT X(1) + Y(4)
150 DATA 2, 1
151 DATA -1, 3
152 DATA 5, 6
153 DATA 2, 4
154 DATA 3, 1
155 DATA 8, 4
156 DATA 5, 1
157 DATA 3, 4
158 DATA 6, 2
159 DATA 1, 1
160 DATA 7, 7
161 DATA 5, 3
170 END
```

Display the program and check to see that you have entered it correctly. Study the program carefully. If we execute the program, what will be typed out?

Execute the program and see whether or not you were right. Record below what was typed out.

3. Type

```
100
```

Now display the program. What has happened?

Execute the program and record what happened.

Does the DIM statement that was originally present in the program appear to be necessary?

---

14. Type

```
100 DIM X(9), Y(9)
110 FOR I = 1 TO 9
```

Display the program. What will happen now if we execute the program?

Try it and see if you were correct.

---

15. Type

```
100
```

Will the program work now that the DIM statement has been taken out?

Try it and record the output.

Compare the results of Step 13 with those of Step 15. Sometimes the DIM statement must be present and other times it need not be. We will return to this question later.

---

6. Clear out the program in memory. Type in the following program:

```
100 DIM A(4,3)
110 FOR I = 1 TO 4
120 FOR J = 1 TO 3
130 READ A(I,J)
140 NEXT J
150 NEXT I
160 FOR I = 1 TO 4
170 FOR J = 1 TO 3
180 PRINT A(I,J);
190 NEXT J
200 PRINT
210 PRINT
220 NEXT I
230 DATA 1, 3, 1
240 DATA 4, 2, 5
250 DATA 1, 4, 2
260 DATA 3, 2, 5
270 END
```

Make sure that you have entered the program correctly, then take a few minutes to study it. Can you see what will be printed out if we execute the program?

Execute the program and record the output.

Compare what was printed out to the numbers in the DATA statements in the program.

7. Clear out the program in memory and then enter the following program:

```
100 DIM A(2,2)
110 FOR I = 1 TO 2
120 INPUT A(I,1),A(I,2)
130 NEXT I
140 PRINT
```

```
150 PRINT
160 FOR I = 1 TO 2
170 FOR J = 1 TO 2
180 PRINT A(I,J);
190 NEXT J
200 PRINT
210 NEXT I
220 END
```

Execute the program and when the INPUT prompt appears, type

```
2,5
3,8
```

What happened?

Compare the output to the numbers you typed in.

18. Clear out the program in memory. Then enter the following program:

```
100 DIM X(3,3)
110 FOR I = 1 TO 3
120 FOR J = 1 TO 3
130 READ X(I,J)
140 NEXT J
150 NEXT I
160 PRINT
170 PRINT
180 FOR I = 1 TO 3
190 FOR J = 1 TO 3
200 PRINT X(I,J);
210 NEXT J
220 PRINT
230 NEXT I
240 DATA 2,1,3
250 DATA 4,7,5
260 DATA 1,2,6
270 END
```

Execute the program. What happened?

Compare the output to the numbers in the DATA statements.

9. This concludes the computer work for this chapter. Turn off the computer.

9–3 DISCUSSION

Usually most students are a bit confused at this point about arrays. Therefore it is important that you pay particular attention to the discussion material to clear up any questions that might have arisen in the computer work.

Single- and Double-Subscripted Variables

The need for subscripted numbers becomes obvious when we must handle large collections of numbers. If, for example, we were writing a program that involved only four numbers, we would have no difficulty naming them. We might call the numbers X, Y, U, and V. But suppose we needed to work with 100 numbers? For this reasons, it is often very useful to have subscripted numbers. Fortunately, BASIC has provisions for subscripts which are ready and waiting for our use.

Consider the following set of numbers:

i	Y_i
1	14
2	8
3	9
4	11
5	16
6	20
7	5
8	3

We can refer to the entire set of numbers with the single name Y. Thus, Y is a collection of numbers, a matrix, or an array-all of which mean roughly the same thing for our purposes. To locate a number in an array, we must have the array name (in this case Y) and the position within the array. Here is where the i column is used. Thus Y(3) (which we read as "Y sub three") locates the third number in the array Y. In this case, Y(3) has the value 9. Likewise, Y(7), is 5, Y(1) is 14, and so on. Most generally we can speak of Y(I) (which would be pronounced "Y sub I"), which denotes any element of the array depending on the value of I. If I were 8, then Y(I) would be 3 in our example. This collection of numbers is one-dimensional, since only one number (subscript) is needed to locate any element in the array.

Next let's look at a two-dimensional array.

$Y_{i,j}$	1	2	3	4
1	3	-1	10	8
2	2	4	5	6
3	1	-2	9	3

Now we need two numbers to locate an element in the array. Given a row number and a column number, we can find any element of the array we desire. For example, Y(1,3) means the element of Y located at row 1, column 3. In the example above, the element has the value 10. In general, we denote an element in the two-dimensional array as Y(I,J). The first subscript (I) is the row number, and the second subscript (J) is the column number.

To make sure you understand how the double subscripts are used, refer to the two-dimensional array in the table above and verify that the following statements are correct:

$$Y_{3,2} = -2$$

$$Y_{1,4} = 8$$

$$Y_{3,3} = 9$$

$$Y_{2,1} = 2$$

An interesting question comes up. Does X(M-N+3,S*T) mean anything? The answer is yes provided that the computer can convert M-N+3 and S*T into numbers. Even Y(Y(1,1),Y(2,3)) is all right as long as the computer can locate the numbers in Y(1,1) and Y(2,3).

However, there is an important point to be remembered. Suppose we want to look up X(A+B) where A = 2.6 and B = 1.1. Thus, A+B = 3.7. But it doesn't make any sense to try to look up the 3.7th number in the array X. Accordingly, the computer will take the integer part of 3.7, and X(A+B) works out to be X(3), the third element in the array X.

■ **Double subscripts define row and column numbers.**

Saving Space for Arrays

The computer must know how big an array is for two reasons. First, there is a question of how much space to save in memory to hold the array. Next, the computer must know the size of the array in order to carry out arithmetic operations properly. Actually, for small arrays, BASIC saves space automatically. If a one-dimensional array is used in a program, BASIC automatically sets up space for ten elements if there is no DIM statement. If a two-dimensional array is used, BASIC will save enough space in memory for a ten by ten array if no DIM statement is in the program. It probably isn't wise to use this feature of BASIC. In this book we will emphasize the routine use of dimension statements in all programs regardless of the size of the arrays.

■ **Save space with a DIM statement.**

An example of a DIM (for "dimension") statement is

```
100 DIM B(5,20),Y(8),Z(34),X(3,6)
```

Four arrays are dimensioned in line 100. B is a two-dimensional array having five rows and twenty columns. Y is one-dimensional, with eight elements. Likewise, Z is one-dimensional, with thirty-four elements. Finally, X is a two-dimensional array with three rows and six columns. It's a good practice to make the DIM statement the first one of the program. This way it is easy to glance at the beginning of the program to see the sizes of the arrays that will be used. At any rate, the DIM statement must be before any other statements that refer to arrays. As indicated above, it is also a good practice to use a DIM statement in all programs.

Subscripted Variables and FOR NEXT Loops.

Since subscripts involve collections of numbers and operations with collections of numbers almost always involve repetition, it seems reasonable that we should employ FOR NEXT statements to handle arrays. We will use FOR NEXT loops to define the subscripts used in the arrays. As an example, the following program segment will set up a six by four array, then load 5s into all the elements.

```
100 DIM A(6,4)
110 FOR R = 1 TO 6
120 FOR C = 1 TO 4
130 LET A(R,C) = 5
140 NEXT C
150 NEXT R
```

If we study this program segment, the details of the process become clear. When line 130 in the program is reached the first time, R = 1 and C = 1. Then R is held constant while C goes to 2, 3, and 4. At each step in this process, the corresponding element of the array is set equal to 5. Then R is set equal to 2, and C takes on the values 1, 2, 3, and 4. The process goes on until all the elements of the array have been set equal to 5.

Either one- or two-dimensional arrays can be handled in this fashion using subscripts. In many applications it is preferable to use FOR NEXT loops to carry out the desired operations on arrays.

9–4 PROGRAM EXAMPLES

The use of subscripted variables permits many interesting problems to be handled easily in BASIC. We will look at several programs to illustrate how subscripts are used.

Example 1 - Examination Grades

To illustrate the concept of a one-dimensional array, let's take an example that is near and dear to the hearts of most students—a set of examination grades. Suppose that we have the following results on an examination given to a class of fifteen students:

Student Number

	1	2	3	4	5	6	7	8	9	10	11	12	13	14	15
Grade	67	82	94	75	48	64	89	91	74	71	65	83	72	69	72

The problem is to write a BASIC program to allow the class grades above to be typed in. The format should appear as follows:

HOW MANY STUDENTS? (You type in)
STUDENT GRADE
1 (You type in grade, etc.)
2
3
(etc.)

The program should compute the class average, the highest grade, and the lowest grade, and print this information out as follows:

CLASS AVERAGE IS (Computer prints out average)
HIGHEST GRADE IS (Computer prints out highest)
LOWEST GRADE IS (Computer prints out lowest grade)

As in past exercises, let's take this by steps. First, since we are going to store the student grades in subscripted form, we must include a DIM statement to save space for the array.

```
100 DIM G(50)
```

We are using the variable G to store grades and can insert up to fifty grades. Next we have a message, an input, and a space.

```
110 PRINT "HOW MANY STUDENTS";
120 INPUT N
130 PRINT
```

Now we are ready to input the grades. First the heading for the table must be generated.

```
140 PRINT "STUDENT", "GRADE"
150 PRINT
```

A loop using FOR NEXT statements is ideal to control the input of grades.

```
160 FOR I = 1 TO N
170 PRINT I,
180 INPUT G(I)
190 NEXT I
```

The student number is printed out in line 170. In line 180, the student number (I) is used as a subscript for the grade. This generates grades in the computer in the form G(1), G(2),...,G(N). The next task is to find the average of the grades. This can be done by summing up all the grades and dividing by the number of grades.

```
200 LET S = 0
210 FOR I = 1 TO N
220 LET S = S+G(I)
230 NEXT I
240 PRINT
```

Now we compute the average and print out the results.

```
250 LET M = S/N
260 PRINT "CLASS AVERAGE IS";M
```

The final part of the program is to locate and print out the highest and lowest grades in the class. H and L will stand for the highest and lowest grades, respectively. Initially we will set both H and L equal to G(1), the first grade in the list. We know that the same grade can't be the highest and lowest at the same time. Thus, we will go through the rest of the grades, compare H and L with each grade, and make adjustments to H and L as required.

```
270 LET H = G(1)
280 LET L = G(1)
290 FOR I = 2 TO N
300 IF L < G(I) THEN 320
310 LET L = G(I)
320 IF H > G(I) THEN 340
330 LET H = G(I)
340 NEXT I
```

The required printout can be obtained with two lines.

```
350 PRINT "HIGHEST GRADE IS";H
360 PRINT "LOWEST GRADE IS";L
```

Finally the END statement completes the program.

```
370 END
```

The complete program follows:

```
100 DIM G(50)
110 PRINT "HOW MANY STUDENTS";
120 INPUT N
130 PRINT
140 PRINT "STUDENT", "GRADE"
150 PRINT
160 FOR I = 1 TO N
170 PRINT I,
180 INPUT G(I)
190 NEXT I
200 LET S = 0
210 LET I = 1 TO N
220 LET S = S+G(I)
230 NEXT I
240 PRINT
250 LET M = S/N
260 PRINT "CLASS AVERAGE IS";M
270 LET H = G(1)
280 LET L = G(1)
290 FOR I = 2 TO N
300 IF L < G(I) THEN 320
310 LET L = G(I)
320 IF H > G(I) THEN 340
330 LET H = G(I)
340 NEXT I
350 PRINT "HIGHEST GRADE IS";H
360 PRINT "LOWEST GRADE IS";L
370 END
```

You should turn on the computer, bring up BASICA and execute this program using the data at the beginning of the discussion.

If you have any difficulty with the highest and lowest search in lines 270 through 340, trace the program in detail.

Example 2 - Course Grades

We can easily extend the ideas in Example 1 to a two-dimensional array. Now, suppose we have a class with ten students, and the course grade is based upon five examinations. Typical results for such a class might be

		Student Number									
		1	2	3	4	5	6	7	8	9	10
	1	92	71	81	52	75	97	100	63	41	75
	2	85	73	79	49	71	91	93	58	52	71
Exam	3	89	74	80	61	79	88	97	55	51	73
	4	96	68	84	58	80	93	95	61	47	70
	5	82	72	82	63	73	92	93	68	56	74

We will use an array with the FOR NEXT statement to READ the data from DATA statements. The computer is to compute and print out the following information:

```
STUDENT            COURSE AVE
1           (Computer prints average, etc.)
2
3
etc.
TEST               CLASS AVE
1           (Computer prints average, etc.)
2
3
etc.
```

The program should start with a DIM statement although the DATA statements can go anywhere in the program.

```
100 DIM G(5,10)
```

This reserves memory space for an array with five rows and ten columns. The row number (R) will be the examination number, and the column number (C) will correspond to the student number.

```
110 DATA 92,71,81,52,75,97,100,63,41,75
120 DATA 85,63,79,49,71,91,93,58,52,71
130 DATA 89,74,80,61,79,88,97,55,51,73
140 DATA 96,68,84,58,80,93,95,61,47,70
150 DATA 82,72,82,63,73,92,93,68,56,74
```

All the numbers can be read into the program with the following FOR NEXT statement.

```
160 FOR R = 1 TO 5
170 FOR C = 1 TO 10
180 READ G(R,C)
190 NEXT C
200 NEXT R
```

This causes the numbers to be read into the matrix G by rows. Thus, the data in line 110 becomes row 1 of the matrix G, and so forth. Before doing anything else, we must print out the required headings.

```
210 PRINT "STUDENT", "COURSE AVE"
220 PRINT
```

Now we can compute the course average for each student.

```
230 FOR C = 1 TO 10
```

Line 230 opens a loop that will look at each column in the matrix. For each value of C, we must compute the column average and print it out.

```
240 LET S = 0
250 FOR R = 1 TO 5
260 LET S = S+G(R,C)
270 NEXT R
280 PRINT C,S/5
```

Then close the C loop.

```
290 NEXT C
```

Now the process is repeated except that the averages are computed on rows rather than columns.

```
300 PRINT
310 PRINT 'TEST, "CLASS AVE"
320 PRINT
330 FOR R = 1 TO 5
340 LET S = 0
350 FOR C = 1 TO 10
360 LET S = S+G(R,C)
370 NEXT C
380 PRINT R,S/10
390 NEXT R
```

Finally the END statement,

```
400 END
```

The complete program follows:

```
100 DIM G(5,10)
110 DATA 92,71,81,52,75,97,100,63,41,75
120 DATA 85,63,79,49,71,91,93,58,52,71
130 DATA 89,74,80,61,79,88,97,55,51,73
140 DATA 96,68,84,58,80,93,95,61,47,70
150 DATA 82,72,82,63,73,92,93,68,56,74
160 FOR R = 1 TO 5
170 FOR C = 1 TO 10
180 READ G(R,C)
190 NEXT C
200 NEXT R
210 PRINT "STUDENT", "COURSE AVE"
220 PRINT
230 FOR C = 1 TO 10
240 LET S = 0
250 FOR R = 1 TO 5
260 LET S = S+G(R,C)
270 NEXT R
280 PRINT C,S/5
290 NEXT C
300 PRINT
310 PRINT "TEST", "CLASS AVE"
320 PRINT
330 FOR R = 1 TO 5
340 LET S = 0
```

```
350 FOR C = 1 TO 10
360 LET S = S + G(R,C)
370 NEXT C
380 PRINT R,S/10
390 NEXT R
400 END
```

This program is an interesting one and illustrates valuable programming techniques involving arrays. It is worth studying and executing on your computer.

Example 3 - *Array Operations*

The final example will consist of a series of short programs that will be given without explanation. Study each program until you are sure you understand what is taking place.

a. Write a program using FOR NEXT loops to load a three by four array with 1s.

```
100 DIM X(3,4)
110 FOR R = 1 TO 3
120 FOR C = 1 TO 4
130 LET X(R,C) = 1
140 NEXT C
150 NEXT R
160 END
```

b. Write a program to generate and load the numbers

2, 4, 8, 16, 32, 64, 128, 256, 512, 1024, 2048

into a one-dimensional array.

```
100 DIM Z(11)
110 LET Z(1) = 2
120 FOR I = 2 TO 11
130 LET Z(I) = 2*Z(I-1)
140 NEXT I
150 END
```

c. Write a program to read in the array

$$\begin{bmatrix} 2 & 3 & 5 \\ 1 & 4 & 2 \end{bmatrix}$$

from DATA statements and then print out the array.

```
100 DIM A(2,3)
110 FOR R = 1 TO 2
120 FOR C = 1 TO 3
130 READ A(R,C)
140 NEXT C
150 NEXT R
160 FOR R = 1 TO 2
170 FOR C = 1 TO 3
180 PRINT A(R,C),
190 NEXT C
200 PRINT
210 NEXT R
220 DATA 2,3,5
230 DATA 1,4,2
240 END
```

9–5 PROBLEMS

1. Write a program using the DATA statements

```
200 DATA 12
210 DATA 2,1,4,3,2,4,5,6,3,5,4,1
```

Which will read the size of an array from the first DATA statement, then read the elements of the array from the second DATA statement, loading them into an array X. Then print out the array.

2. Write a program to fill a 3 by 4 array with ones.

3. Write a program to call for the input of a square N by N matrix where N is a whole number no larger than 10. Compute and print out the sum of the entries on the main diagonal of the array.

4. Write a BASIC program using the READ command to read twenty-five numbers from the DATA statements into a one-dimensional array named A. Search the array and print out the number of elements in the array that are greater than fifty. Fill in the required DATA statements with any numbers you choose.

5. Write a program to call for the input of a M by N matrix. Assume that both M and N are no larger than 15. Then compute and print out the sum of all the elements in the matrix.

6. The program below is supposed to compute and print out the sum of the elements in a one-dimensional array that are positive but not greater than 10. As it stands the program is incorrect. What's wrong?

```
100 DIM A(6)
110 FOR I = 1 TO 6
120 INPUT A(I)
130 NEXT I
140 LET S = 0
150 FOR I = 6 TO 1 STEP -1
160 IF A(I) > 10 THEN 180
170 LET S = S+A(I)
180 NEXT I
190 PRINT S
200 END
```

7. What will be output if the following program is executed?

```
100 DIM Y(6)
110 FOR I = 1 TO 6
120 READ Y(I)
130 NEXT I
140 DATA 2,1,3,1,2,1
150 LET S1 = 0
160 LET S2 = 0
170 FOR I = 1 TO 6
180 LET S1 = S1 + Y(I)
190 LET S2 = S2 + Y(I)^2
200 NEXT I
210 LET X = S2 - S1
220 PRINT X
230 END
```

8. What will be output if the following program is executed?

```
100 DIM A(10)
110 FOR I = 1 TO 10
120 READ A(I)
130 NEXT I
140 LET S = A(1)
150 FOR I = 1 TO 9
160 LET A(I) = A(I+1)
170 NEXT I
180 LET A(10) = S
190 FOR I = 1 TO 10
200 PRINT A(I)
210 NEXT I
220 DATA 10,9,8,7,6,5,4,3,2,1
230 END
```

9. What will be printed out if the following program is executed?

```
100 DIM X(4,4)
110 FOR I = 1 TO 4
120 FOR J = 1 TO 4
130 READ X(I,J)
140 NEXT J
150 NEXT I
160 DATA 1,2,3,4,2,3,4,5
170 DATA 3,4,5,6,4,5,6,7
180 LET S = 0
190 FOR I = 1 TO 4
200 LET S = S+X(I,5-I)
210 NEXT I
220 PRINT S
230 END
```

10. What will be printed out if the following program is executed?

```
100 DIM Y(4,4)
110 FOR R = 1 TO 4
120 FOR C = 1 TO 4
130 LET Y(R,C) = 0
140 NEXT C
150 NEXT R
```

```
160 FOR R = 1 TO 4
170 FOR C = 1 TO 4
180 LET Y(R,C) = R*C
190 NEXT C
200 NEXT R
210 FOR R = 1 TO 4
220 FOR C = 1 TO 4
230 PRINT Y(R,C);
240 NEXT C
250 PRINT
260 NEXT R
270 END
```

. Write a BASIC program to call for the input of N (assumed to be a whole number between 1 and 100), then input a one-dimensional array with N elements. Sort the array into descending order, and finally print out the sorted array.

. Let's assume that the first number in the DATA statements gives the number of pieces of data to follow. Assume that the pieces of data are all whole numbers between 1 and 10 inclusive. Write a program that will compute the number of 1s and 2s etc., in the data and then print this out. (Hint: use the data as they are read in as a subscript to increment an element of an array used to count the numbers.)

. What will be printed out if the following program is executed?

```
100 DIM Z(6,6)
110 FOR R = 1 TO 6
120 FOR C = 1 TO 6
130 LET Z(R,C) = 0
140 NEXT C
150 NEXT R
160 FOR R = 1 TO 5 STEP 2
170 FOR C = R TO 6
180 LET Z(R, C) = 1
190 NEXT C
200 NEXT R
210 FOR R = 1 TO 6
220 FOR C = 1 TO 6
230 PRINT Z(R,C);
240 NEXT C
250 PRINT
```

```
260 NEXT R
270 END
```

14. If the program below is executed, what will the computer print out?

```
100 DIM A(5,5)
110 FOR R = 1 TO 5
120 FOR C = 1 TO 5
130 READ A(R,C)
140 NEXT C
150 NEXT R
160 DATA 2,2,2,2,2,2,2,2,2,2
170 DATA 2,2,2,2,2,2,2,2,2,2
180 DATA 2,2,2,2,2
190 FOR C = 5 TO 1 STEP -1
200 FOR R = 1 TO C
210 LET A(R,C) = 3
220 NEXT R
230 NEXT C
240 FOR R = 1 TO 5
250 FOR C = 1 TO 5
260 PRINT A(R,C);
270 NEXT C
280 PRINT
290 NEXT R
300 END
```

15. Write a program to read the following array from DATA statements, then print out the array.

$$\begin{bmatrix} 2 & 1 & 0 & 5 & 1 \\ 3 & 2 & 1 & 3 & 1 \end{bmatrix}$$

16. Write a program to read the following array from DATA statements, then print out the array.

$$\begin{bmatrix} 5 & 3 \\ 2 & 0 \\ -1 & 1 \\ 4 & 2 \\ 2 & 6 \end{bmatrix}$$

Write a BASIC program that will call for the input of an M by N array. Then compute and print out the sum of the elements in each row and the product of the elements in each column.

Write a BASIC program that will read two arrays from DATA statements. Both the arrays are two by three. Then compute a third two by three array such that each element is the sum of the corresponding elements in the first two arrays. Print out the third array.

The data below represent sales totals made by salespersons over a one-week period.

		Mon	Tue	Wed	Thu	Fri	Sat
Salesperson	1	48	40	73	120	100	90
	2	75	130	90	40	110	85
	3	50	72	140	125	106	92
	4	108	75	92	152	91	87

Write a program that will compute and print out
a. The daily sales totals
b. The weekly sales totals for each salesperson
c. The total weekly sales

Write a program to call for the input of a 4 by 4 matrix. Compute a new matrix from the first with the rows and columns interchanged. That is, row 1 of the input matrix becomes column 1 of the new matrix. Row 2 of the input matrix becomes column 2 of the new matrix, and so on. Print out the new matrix.

Consider the two arrays below:

P	X
1	28
5	2
3	14
4	3
2	17
6	9

Each element of P "points" to an element of X. P(1) = 1 and X(1) = 28. P(2) = 5 and X(5) = 17. If you keep this process up, the values of X are listed in descending order. Write a program to set up two arrays X and P to some convenient length. Then call for the input of arbitrary values of X from the keyboard. Construct the array P so that its elements point to X in descending order as illustrated above. Then print out the two arrays as shown.

9–6 PRACTICE TEST

Check yourself with the following practice test. The answers are given at the end of the book.

1. What is the purpose of the DIM statement?

____

2. We have an array named X. What variable name does BASIC use to locate the element in row 3, column 4?

____

3. Use an array in a progam to input a list of numbers, then find and print out the sum of the positive numbers in the list. The printout should look as follows:

   HOW MANY NUMBERS? (You type in the number)
   WHAT ARE THE NUMBERS? (You type them in)
   THE SUM OF POSITIVE ELEMENTS IS (Computer types out answer)

4. Write a program using FOR NEXT statements to load a four by six array with 4s.

____

5. What will be printed out if the following program is executed?

```
100 DIM A(5,5)
110 FOR I = 1 TO 5
120 FOR J = 1 TO 5
130 LET A(R,C) = 0
140 NEXT J
150 NEXT I
160 FOR I = 1 TO 5
```

```
170 LET A(I,I) = 2
180 NEXT I
190 FOR I = 1 TO 5
200 FOR J = 1 TO 5
210 PRINT A(I,J);
220 NEXT J
230 PRINT
240 NEXT I
250 END
```

The following array is named A:

$$\begin{bmatrix} 1 & 3 & 5 \\ 6 & 2 & 4 \end{bmatrix}$$

a. Write a DIM statement for A.

b. What is the value of A(2,3)?

c. If X = 1 and Y = 2, what is A(X,Y)?

d. What is A(A(1,1),A(2,2))?

CHAPTER 10

STRING VARIABLES

10—1 OBJECTIVES

Some of the most important applications of computers are non-numeric and deal with characters rather than numbers. Strings of characters can be handled as "string variables" and are the subject of this chapter. Specifically we will look at the following string-related topics.

String Input and Output

Before meaningful operations can be carried out on strings we must learn how input and output of string variables are handled on the computer.

String Functions

You have already studied BASIC functions that operated on numbers. Now we will turn to functions which work on strings of characters.

String Operations

The final goal is to write programs which work with string variables.

10—2 DISCOVERY EXERCISES

The manipulation of character strings expands the capabilities of our computer programs beyond simple numerical computations.

Computer Work

1. Turn on the computer and bring up BASICA. Enter the following program:

```
100 INPUT A$
110 PRINT
120 PRINT A$
130 PRINT A$
140 END
```

The A$ in the program identifies the variable as a string variable. Execute the program and at the input prompt (the question mark) type in your full name. What happened?

---

2. Now modify the program as follows:

```
100 INPUT A$,B$
110 PRINT
120 PRINT B$
130 PRINT A$
140 END
```

If you execute the program and at the input prompt type the words INTELLIGENT and CONVERSATION separated by a comma what do you think will be printed back?

Try it and record what did happen.

Let's try a different variation. Clear out the program and enter the following:

```
100 READ X,X$,Y,Y$
110 DATA 10,"HERB",20,"CHARLIE"
120 PRINT X,Y
130 PRINT X$,Y$
140 END
```

This program contains several new ideas. What do you think will happen if you execute the program?

OK, execute the program and record what took place.

Now that you have seen that strings can be included in DATA statements, we should go a bit further. Change line 100 to read

```
100 READ X$,X,Y,Y$
```

What will happen if you try to execute the program in this form?

See if you were right. Record below what took place when you tried to execute the program.

5. Clearly, you must be careful to ensure that the type of information in the DATA statements matches the type of variable in READ statements. Now on to a different topic. Clear out the program and enter the following:

```
100 INPUT C$
110 LET N = LEN(C$)
120 PRINT N
130 END
```

The new feature in this program is the function LEN(C$). It is new because it works on a string (in this case the string is C$) rather than a number. Can you guess what the function does?

____

Notice that the result of the function LEN operating on a string must be a number since the result is assigned to a numeric variable N.

6. Execute the program and at the input prompt type in ABCDE. What was printed back?

____

Try it again, but this time type in AARDVARK. What happened?

____

By now you should have a pretty good idea what the LEN function does.

7. Here's a new problem for you. If you execute the program and at the input prompt merely press the ENTER key what do you think will be printed back by the computer?

____

Try it out and see if you were correct. Now just one more variation. Execute the program and at the input prompt type in R O B E R T. Note the spaces between the characters. What was typed back?

____

In the LEN function, do spaces count as characters?

Next we want to be able to specify a substring in a given string. That is, given a string A$ how can we specify M characters of that string starting with the Nth character in that string? The function that gives this substring is MID$(A$,N,M). It gives M characters from A$ starting at the Nth character.

Now clear out the program in memory and enter the one below:

```
100 INPUT A$
110 PRINT "M = ";
120 INPUT M
130 PRINT "N = ";
140 INPUT N
150 PRINT MID$(A$,N,M)
160 END
```

Execute the program and at the input prompt for the string type MISSISSIPPI. Note that the length of this string is 11. Enter 5 for M and 4 for N. What happened?

You should have seen the substring SISSI typed out.

Clear out the program from memory and enter the one below:

```
100 INPUT A$
110 INPUT I
120 PRINT MID$(A$,I,1)
130 PRINT
140 GOTO 110
150 END
```

Execute the program and at the first input prompt type in ABCDEFGHIJKLMNOPQRSTUVWXYZ. At the second input prompt type in 20. What happened?

The computer is at the input prompt for I. This time, type in 10. What happened?

Experiment with various values of I between 1 and 26. Describe in your own words what happens when the computer is directed to print out MID$(A$,I,1).

11. There is one last thing to check. You should still be at the input prompt for I. Type in 30. What happened?

By now you should understand fairly clearly what happens when the computer prints out MID$(A$,I,1). Of course, in this instance, the value of I is greater than the length of the string. We will return to this topic in the discussion section. Jump your computer out of the input loop.

12. Experiment on your own with this program. Try various strings and different values of M and N until you understand exactly how the MID$ function works.

13. Now on to a different topic. Clear out the program in memory and enter the following:

```
100 INPUT A$
110 INPUT B$
120 IF A$ < B$ THEN 150
130 PRINT B$
140 GOTO 100
150 PRINT A$
160 GOTO 100
170 END
```

Take a few moments to study the program. Clearly, the interesting part is in line 120 where the strings A$ and B$ are involved in an IF THEN statement. In particular, what do you suppose A$ < B$ means with regard to strings?

The way to find out if you are right or not is to execute the program and run a few test cases through the computer. Execute the program and at the first input prompt, type in DUCK; at the second prompt, type in CHICKEN. What was typed out?

____

4. The computer is at the input prompt waiting for a string to be typed in. This time type in HOUSE followed by TELEVISION. What was typed out?

____

Keep experimenting with words or letters of your choice until you see exactly what the expression A$ < B$ means. Once you understand this it should be easy for you to see what A$ = B$, A$ > = B$, or A$ <> B$ would mean.

5. Jump the computer out of the input loop. Clear out the program in memory. Let's go on to the next string variable statement.

CHR$ is the function that converts a position number in the set of characters the computer uses to the corresponding character.

6. Enter the following program:

```
100 INPUT N
110 PRINT CHR$(N)
120 GOTO 100
130 END
```

Now execute the program and at the input prompt, type in 65. What happened?

____

The program will keep looping through as long as we desire. This time try 66. What happened?

____

You may wish to try 49, 50, and 236 also.

17. By now, the cat should be out of the bag. Play with this program trying out various numerical inputs. Keep the numbers in the range 1 to 255. Very quickly, you should see that you can refer to a character either by the character itself or by a position number in the set of characters.

18. To see a portion of the ASCII character set, clear out the memory and type in the following program.

```
100 FOR N = 65 TO 122
110 PRINT CHR$(N);"  ";
120 NEXT N
130 END
```

You can see the entire ASCII character set by referring to Appendix G of the *BASIC* reference manual.

19. Now on to a different topic. First, clear out the program in memory. ASC is the function that converts a character to the equivalent position number in the character set used by the computer.

Type in the following program:

```
100 INPUT A$
110 LET X = ASC(A$)
120 PRINT X
130 GOTO 100
140 END
```

Execute the program and at the input prompt, type Z. What happened?

____

This new function, ASC(A$), is just the reverse of CHR$(N). Use various letters and numbers and compare your results to those you obtained in Step 17.

20. There is one more detail to be seen to. Your computer should still be at the input prompt waiting for A$ to be typed in. This time type in POTATO. Note what was typed back. Then try PEA. What happened?

____

The only similarity between the two words is that they both have the same first letter. We will return to this concept later.

This concludes the computer work for this chapter. Turn off the computer and go on to the next section.

10—3 DISCUSSION

Now let's go back over the ideas introduced in the computer work.

String Input and Output

As you have already seen, a set of characters surrounded by quotation marks is called a string. The quotation marks are not part of the string however. The new idea in this chapter is that the string can be treated as a variable — the string variable.

First, the string variable is identified by appending a dollar sign ($) to a name. Thus, BARN$, BOX$, and B$ are string variable names.

Input and output of string variables is handled the same way as for numeric variables. We can mix numeric and string variables in the same BASIC statements. Examples might be

```
100 PRINT A$,X,Y,Z$
110 INPUT M$,N
120 READ A$,B$,Z
```

You must be careful that the input in either INPUT or READ statements matches the type of variable given. In line 110 above, the computer would be looking for a string of characters and a number. However, you must be aware that you can type in 123456789 and if the computer is looking for a string it will identify this quantity as a string, not as a number. The reason is that the string, as has been pointed out, consists of characters, and symbols 0 through 9 are part of the standard character set that will be discussed later. If, on the other hand, the computer is looking for a number and you type in ABCDEFGHI, you will get an error.

String Functions

The LEN function is used to determine the length of a string. If, for example, A$ = "HOW NOW BROWN COW" then LEN(A$) = 17. Note that the spaces are counted as characters. You can also have a "null" string. If A$ = "" (there is nothing inside the quotation marks), then LEN(A$) = 0.

■ **LEN(A$) gives the number of characters in A$.**

A substring is a piece or segment of a string. There are several ways to deal with substrings. Consider the following program:

```
100 LET A$ = "ROBERT E. LEE"
110 PRINT MID$(A$,8,6)
120 END
```

The expression MID$(A$,8,6) identifies the substring of A$ consisting of six characters starting at the eighth character. If the program were run, the characters E. LEE would be printed out.

■ **MID$(A$,I,J) gives J characters of string A$ starting at character I.**

String variables can be compared in IF THEN statements. The comparison is done by alphabetical ordering. Thus A ⟨ B since A comes before B in the alphabet. CAT ⟨ DOG, HOUSE ⟩ CAR, PEA ⟨ PEARL, and so on.

The final topic that we will discuss concerns the ASCII (short for American Standard Code for Information Interchange) standard character set. This set is used on most computers and consists of one-hundred and twenty-eight characters numbered 0 through 127. Refer to your *BASIC* reference manual for a complete listing of the ASCII character set.

Characters 0 through 31 are special purpose and have no relevancy to our discussion. The upper-case letters A through Z are numbered 65 through 90. The lower-case letters a through z are numbered 97 through 122. The numerals 0 through 9 are numbered 48 through 57. The other numbered characters include punctuation marks, arithmetic operators (+, −, *, etc.) and other special characters.

Two string functions work with the ASCII character set. First, CHR$(N) returns the Nth character from the ASCII character set. For example, CHR$(65) = "A", CHR$(122) = "z", and so forth. We can also turn things around and convert from a character to its ASCII number. This is done with the ASC(A$) function. For example, ASC(A) = 65 and ASC(z) = 122.

Suppose that A$ = "AIRPLANE". What is ASC(A$)? Since the length of the string is greater than one, only the first character is considered. In this case the first character is A and ASC(A$) = 65.

10–4 PROGRAM EXAMPLES

Several example programs should help you pull together the various concepts about strings that have been introduced in this chapter.

Example 1 - String Reversal

The task is to write a program to call for the input of a string and then print it back in reverse order. First, we must arrange for the string input.

```
100 INPUT A$
```

The next few lines print the string back in reverse order.

```
110 FOR X = LEN(A$) TO 1 STEP -1
120 PRINT MID$(A$,X,1);
130 NEXT X
```

The loop steps backwards from the length of the string to 1. The function MID$(A$,X,1) identifies the substring in A$ consisting of 1 character starting at character number X. This isolates a single character.

With an END statement added the complete program is

```
100 INPUT A$
110 FOR X = LEN(A$) TO 1 STEP -1
120 PRINT MID$(A$,X,1);
130 NEXT X
140 END
```

You may wish to run this program using your own name as input.

Example 2 - Word Count

The number of words in a sentence can be determined from the number of spaces (assuming that the only purpose of a space is to separate words). The following program prints out the number of words in the input string.

```
100 INPUT A$
110 LET S = 0
120 FOR I = 1 TO LEN(A$)
130 IF MID$(A$,I,1) <> " " THEN 150
140 LET S = S+1
150 NEXT I
160 PRINT 'WORD COUNT = ",S+1
170 END
```

Study the program until you see exactly how it works. Try out the program by typing in a sentence. Verify that it works correctly.

Example 3 - Replacement Code

Suppose we want a program to encode a sentence. A simple-minded way to construct a code (which incidentally could be broken very rapidly with computers) is to replace each character in the message with another. This is done most easily by reference to the ASCII character set. However, let's do this one "from scratch."

The first part of the program calls for the input of the string to be coded and sets up the conversion scheme.

```
100 LET B$ = "ABCDEFGHIJKLMNOPQRSTUVWXYZ ,."
110 LET C$ = "ETAVZBHCW KPSYDF,GXIMJLONQU.R"
120 INPUT A$
```

B$ contains the characters that can be used in the input string which is to be coded. C$ is the replacement key. An A in the input string is to be replaced by an E, F is replaced by B, J by a space, and so on.

Now we can examine each character and do the replacement.

```
130 FOR I = 1 TO LEN(A$)
140 FOR J = 1 TO 29
150 IF MID$(A$,I,1) <> MID$(B$,J,1) THEN 180
160 PRINT MID$(C$,J,1);
170 GOTO 190
180 NEXT J
190 NEXT I
```

The outer I loop steps through each character in A$. The inner J loop compares the Ith character of A$ to the character in B$ until a match is found at the Jth character. When this happens, the coded Jth character of C$ is printed out and the program goes on to the next character in A$.

We finish the program with

```
200 PRINT
210 END
```

The complete program is

```
100 LET B$ = "ABCDEFGHIJKLMNOPQRSTUVWXYZ ,."
110 LET C$ = "ETAVZBHCW KPSYDF,GXIMJLONQU.R"
120 INPUT A$
130 FOR I = 1 TO LEN(A$)
140 FOR J = 1 TO 29
150 IF MID$(A$,I,1) <> MID$(B$,J,1) THEN 180
160 PRINT MID$(C$,J,1);
170 GOTO 190
180 NEXT J
190 NEXT I
200 PRINT
210 END
```

The code can be changed by rearranging the characters in C$. It might be interesting for you to try out the program and see how a coded message looks. Be sure to use the Caps Lock key to insure that only capital letters are entered.

10–5 PROBLEMS

1. Write a program to call for the input of a string. Then print the string out in a vertical column of characters.

2. Write a program to call for the input of a string. Then print the string back diagonally down and across the page so that each character is one line below and one character to the right of the previous character.

3. Write a program to count the number of vowels in an input string.

4. Write a program to call for the input of a string. Then print the words in the string in a vertical column.

5. Ask for a sentence to be input. Generate a new string from this sentence that has all the spaces removed. Then print out the new string.

6. Write a program to call for the input of a string consisting of upper-case letters. Then convert all the upper-case letters to lower-case and print the string back. You may need to refer to the ASCII character set in your *BASIC* reference manual, Appendix G.

7. Assume that five sentences are to be typed in one at a time. Write a program to count the number of times the word THE appears in the five sentences.

8. If at the input prompt for the program below you type in the string ABCDEFGH what will be output?

```
100 INPUT A$
110 FOR J = 1 TO LEN(A$) STEP 2
120 PRINT MID$(A$,J,1);
130 NEXT J
140 END
```

9. Write a program to call for the input of a string. Count the number of times the character I is followed by the character N.

. We want to count the frequency of occurrence of each of the 26 letters in the alphabet (you may assume that they are all upper-case) in ten sentences to be typed in at the keyboard. Do not count spaces or punctuation marks. Write a program to compute and print out a table consisting of each of the letters and the number of times it occurred in the sentences. Do you think you could identify an author with the use of such a table?

10–6 PRACTICE TEST

Take the following test to see how well you have mastered the chapter. The answers are at the end of the book.

. How are string variables identified in BASIC?

____

. If A$ = "KITTY" and B$ = "KITTYCAT" then A$ > B$. True or false?

____

. If A$ = "HOW NOW BROWN COW" write a function that will extract NOW BROWN.

____

. Write a program to call for the input of a string and then keep printing back the string with one character deleted each time until nothing is left. If, for example, you typed in PIECE OF CAKE, the computer should print out

```
PIECE OF CAKE
PIECE OF CAK
PIECE OF CA
PIECE OF C
PIECE OF
PIECE OF
PIECE O
PIECE
PIECE
PIEC
PIE
PI
P
```

5. What will be printed out if the following program is executed?

```
100 FOR N = 97 TO 122
110 FOR M = 97 TO N
120 PRINT CHR$(M);
130 NEXT M
140 PRINT
150 NEXT N
160 END
```

CHAPTER 11

"DO-IT-YOURSELF" FUNCTIONS AND SUBROUTINES

11—1 OBJECTIVES

In this chapter we will learn how the computer can be programmed to perform suboperations. This can be done through either program segments or special on-line instructions. Specifically, we will look at the following things.

"Do-It-Yourself" Functions

We have previously seen functions that are built into BASIC. Now we will learn how to define our own functions to carry out any desired task.

Subroutines

When complicated operations are to be repeated, often subroutines are very useful. We will explore how subroutines can be set up and used in BASIC programs.

Program Applications

Sometimes it is difficult for the beginner to see the value of user-defined functions and subroutines. These ideas will be stressed in our continued attention to programming in BASIC.

11–2 DISCOVERY EXERCISES

Computer Work

1. Turn on the computer and bring up BASICA.
Enter the following program:

```
100 DEF FNA(X) = 5*X+4
110 LET X = 2
120 LET Y = 5*X+4
130 PRINT Y,FNA(2)
140 END
```

Execute the program and record the output below.

____

2. Type

```
130 PRINT Y,FNA(X)
```

Display the program in memory. What do you think will happen if we execute this program?

____

Execute the program. What did happen?

____

3. Type

```
110 LET X = 5
```

Display the program and study it. Now what will be output if we execute the program?

____

See if you were right. Execute the program and record what happened.

____

4. Type

```
130 PRINT Y,FNA(5)
```

Display the program. What do you think the program will do now?

____

Execute the program and write down the output.

____

5. Notice that the expressions after the equal signs in lines 100 and 120 of your program are the same. In one of the versions of the program, we printed out Y and FNA(X) and saw that they were the same. Let's follow up on this information. Clear out the program in memory. Then enter the following program:

```
100 DEF FNA(X) = X^2
110 DEF FNB(X) = 3*X
120 DEF FNC(X) = X+2
130 LET X = 1
140 PRINT FNA(X),FNB(X),FNC(X)
150 END
```

Study the program carefully. What do you think will be printed out if the program is executed?

____

Now execute the program and write down what happened.

____

Without changing your program, what do you think will happen if you substitute 1 for X in the expressions on the right side of lines 100, 110, and 120 and then execute the program. Write down the numbers you would obtain.

____

Now compare these numbers to those typed out by the computer.

6. Type

```
130 LET X = 2
```

Display the program. What will be printed out by the program if it is executed now?

____

See if you were right. Execute the program and record the results below.

____

7. Type

```
130 LET X = 3
```

Now what will happen if the program is executed?

____

Verify your answer by executing the program and recording what happened.

____

8. Now on to some more ideas we can explore with this program. Type

```
130 LET X = 1
140 PRINT FNC(X+4),FNA(X),FNB(2)
```

Display the program. Write down what you think will be printed out if the program is executed.

____

Execute the program and record the output.

____

9. Let's try a slightly different variation on the theme we have been exploring. Type

```
140 PRINT FNA(X),FNB(FNA(X))
```

Display the program and study it carefully. Try to figure out what will be printed out when the program is executed. Record your answer below.

Execute the program and see if you were right. Write down below what happened.

0. One last point on this matter. Type

```
130 LET X = 4
140 PRINT FNA(X),FNC(X),FNA(SQR(X))
```

Now what will happen in the program?

Execute the program and record what happened?

1. Clear out the program in memory. Enter the following program:

```
100 PRINT "A";
110 GOSUB 200
120 PRINT "B";
130 GOSUB 300
140 PRINT "C";
150 END
200 PRINT 1;
210 RETURN
300 PRINT 2;
310 RETURN
```

This program has two new statements that you haven't seen so far. They are GOSUB and RETURN. The program itself is intended only to provide practice in tracing these new statements. Execute the program and record the output.

____

Compare what was printed out with the program lines that caused the printout.

____

12. The GOSUB statement in line 110 transfers the program to which statement? (Hint: Look at the printout in Step 11.)

____

13. The RETURN statement in line 210 transfers the program to which statement? (Hint: Again, examine the printout in Step 11.)

____

14. The line numbers below indicate the flow of the program as it is executed.

Line Number	What Happens
100	Print out A
110	Transfer to line 200
200	Print out 1
210	Transfer to line 120
120	Print out B
130	Transfer to line 300
300	Print out 2
310	Transfer to line 140
140	Print out C
150	End of program

Study this carefully and follow through with the program. Can you see the purpose of the GOSUB and RETURN statements yet? What about the placement of the END statement?

Clear out the program in memory. Enter the following program:

```
100 REM PROGRAM TO DEMONSTRATE SUBROUTINES
110 DIM X(4)
120 FOR I = 1 TO 4
130 READ X(I)
140 NEXT I
150 REM SORT
160 GOSUB 300
170 REM PRINT OUT SORTED ARRAY
180 FOR I = 1 TO 4
190 PRINT X(I),
200 NEXT I
210 PRINT
220 LET X(3) = 7
230 REM SORT AGAIN
240 GOSUB 300
250 REM PRINT OUT SORTED ARRAY
260 FOR I = 1 TO 4
270 PRINT X(I),
280 NEXT I
290 END
295 DATA 2,1,5,6
300 REM SUBROUTINE TO SORT
310 FOR I = 1 TO 3
320 IF X(I+1) > X(I) THEN 370
330 LET C = X(I+1)
340 LET X(I+1) = X(I)
350 LET X(I) = C
360 GOTO 310
370 NEXT I
380 RETURN
```

Display the program and check that you have entered it correctly. This program furnishes an example of how a subroutine might be used. The subroutine in lines 300 through 380 sorts the array X into ascending order. Execute the program and record the output.

____

Note that the original array is

```
2 1 5 6
```

You can see this by checking the DATA statement in line 295. In line 160, the program jumps to the subroutine and a sort of the numbers is done. After the program returns to line 170, the sorted array is now

```
1 2 5 6
```

In line 220, we change the third element of the array, then branch to the subroutine for another sorting. After the return to line 250, the sorted array

```
1 2 6 7
```

is printed out. Finally, the END command in line 290 causes the program to stop executing. Clearly, we could sort the array X as often as desired by merely inserting a statement GOSUB 300. This is certainly more efficient that writing out the instructions for sorting each time it is desired.

16. Now let us look at another statement. Clear out the memory and type the following program.

```
100 PRINT "ENTER A NUMBER BETWEEN 1 AND 5.
110 PRINT "ENTER 5 TO QUIT."
120 INPUT N
130 ON N GOSUB 1000,2000,3000,4000
140 IF N=5 THEN END ELSE 100
```

```
1000 PLAY "C"
1010 RETURN
2000 PLAY "DD"
2010 RETURN
3000 PLAY "EEE"
3010 RETURN
4000 PLAY "FFFF"
4010 RETURN
```

What note(s) will be played if you enter 3?

Run the program. Were you right?

. This completes the computer work for this chapter. Turn off the computer.

11–3 DISCUSSION

Now we need to examine the ideas introduced in the computer work. Once you understand clearly how the computer handles these ideas, you will have powerful new skills to use in your programs.

"Do-It-Yourself" Functions

The DEF (an abbreviation for "define") statement permits us to have user-specified functions in BASIC programs in addition to those functions (SQR, INT, etc.) already built into the language. The form of all DEF statements is the same.

⟨line #⟩ **DEF FN**⟨letter⟩⟨variable⟩ = ⟨expression using variable⟩

```
100 DEF FNP(X) = X^2 - 3*X
```

Since there are twenty-six letters in the alphabet that could follow FN, we could conceivably have twenty-six defined functions in a single program.

If the DEF statement in line 100 were used in a program, and later on the expression FNP(2) were used, the computer would identify that FNP was defined in line 100 and would then substitute

2 for X on the right side of the equal sign in the DEF statement, with the result that

$$FNP(2) = -2$$

Likewise, if TIME = 5, then

$$FNP(TIME) = 10$$

The built-in functions in BASIC may be used in the DEF statements. For example,

```
100 DEF FNB(Y) = SQR(Y^1.5)+3*Y
```

is OK. Furthermore, you may use other defined functions in a DEF statement. For example,

```
100 DEF FNB(Y) = FNA(Y) + SQR(Y)
```

is correct provided the function FNA has previously been defined.

The primary purpose of the user-specified functions that are set up with the DEF statements is to simplify programming by avoiding repeated use of complicated expressions. The wise programmer should be alert for opportunities to save effort with the use of DEF statements.

■ **Define your own functions with a DEF statement.**

Subroutines

A limitation of the DEF statements is that it can be no more than a single line. More complicated situations in which we want to carry out the same process many times in a program are bound to come up. That is where subroutines are very useful. The diagram below indicates how a subroutine might be used in a program.

Main program begins	____________________
	____________________
	____________________
	200 GOSUB 1000
	210
	____________________
	____________________
	____________________
	350 GOSUB 1000
	360
	____________________
Main program ends	430 END
Subroutine begins	1000 REM SUBROUTINE
	____________________
	____________________
	____________________
End of subroutine	1150 RETURN

If the typical program above were executed, when the computer reached the GOSUB in line 200, the program would jump to the beginning of the subroutine in line 1000. The subroutine would be executed, and when the RETURN was encountered in line 1150, control would be passed to the next higher line number after the GOSUB that put us in the subroutine. In this case the program would jump back to line 210. Then the computer would proceed through the main program to the GOSUB in line 350, which would again branch control to the subroutine in line 1000. This time the RETURN would jump back in the program to line 360.

Of course, we could have used GOSUB 1000 as many times as we wanted in the program or could have had as many subroutines as needed. Generally, the top part of the program is the main program and the subroutines are grouped together at the end. There is a good reason for this. We want to perform the subroutines only when they are called by a GOSUB. Thus, after the main program is finshed we put an END statement in the program.

■ **Transfer <u>to</u> subroutines with GOSUB.**

It is possible, and sometimes desirable, to jump to a subroutine from a subroutine. The diagram below indicates how the computer treats such an event.

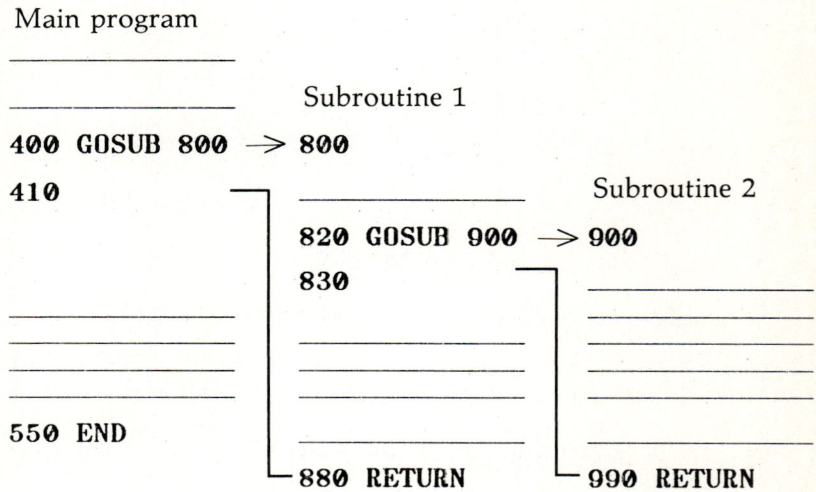

Note that the control passes from 400 to 800, on down to 820, to 900, and on down to the RETURN in line 990. Of course, the question here is, Does the RETURN take us back to line 410 or line 830? The answer is determined by the rule that the RETURN takes us back to the next statement after the GOSUB that put us in the subroutine containing the RETURN. We are in subroutine 2 because of the GOSUB in line 820; hence the RETURN in line 990 branches us back to line 830. The same rule applies when we reach the RETURN in line 880. At that point we are in subroutine 1 and arrived there from the GOSUB in line 400. Thus, the RETURN in line 880 carries us back to line 410.

- **Get back from subroutines with RETURN**

The ON...GOSUB statement allows numerous subroutines to be called based upon the value of a numeric variable. For example, the statement

```
140 ON N GOSUB 300,400,500
```

will go to the subroutine at 300 if N is 1, to the subroutine at 400 if N is 2, or to the subroutine at 500 if N is 3.

At this point it may not be clear to you why subroutines are valuable. The need for subroutines becomes more evident as you acquire more skill as a programmer. It is enough at this time to point out that subroutines are extrememly important and are considered to be one of the most powerful tools available to the programmer.

11—4 PROGRAM EXAMPLES

Several programs should assist you to master the ideas involved in both user-defined functions and subroutines.

Example 1 - Rounding Off Dollar Values to Cents

Business applications generally involve printing out the results of calculations in dollars and cents. Since the computer normally handles seven significant figures, we might get an amount like 23.15793 typed out. This looks strange, and to solve the problem we should round off the figure to the nearest cent, or 23.16.

This is an ideal application for a user-defined function. Let's write a program that will produce the following output when executed:

```
LABEL PRICE? (You type in price)
10% DISCOUNT IS (Computer prints discount price)
15% DISCOUNT IS (Computer prints discount price)
20% DISCOUNT IS (Computer prints discount price)
```

All dollar values typed out should be rounded off to the nearest cent.

First we must define a function to do the rounding. Such a function is

```
100 DEF FNR(X) = INT(X*100+.5)/100
```

To see how this rule works, suppose X = 23.1597. We can follow this value through the expression to see what happens.

$$
\begin{aligned}
X*100 &= 2315.97\\
X*100+0.5 &= 2316.47\\
INT(X*100+0.5) &= 2316\\
INT(X*100+0.5)/100 &= 23.16
\end{aligned}
$$

Therefore 23.1597 was correctly rounded up to 23.16.

As a second example, suppose that X = 23.1547. Then

$$
\begin{aligned}
X*100 &= 2315.47\\
X*100+0.5 &= 2315.97\\
INT(X*100+0.5) &= 2315\\
INT(X*100+0.5)/100 &= 23.15
\end{aligned}
$$

with the result that 23.1547 was correctly rounded down to 23.15.

The next few lines of the program are self-explanatory.

```
110 PRINT "LABEL PRICE"
120 INPUT Z
130 PRINT "10% DISCOUNT IS";FNR(.9*Z)
140 PRINT "15% DISCOUNT IS";FNR(.85*Z)
150 PRINT "20% DISCOUNT IS";FNR(.8*Z)
```

If desired, we can loop back to the beginning with

```
160 GOTO 110
```

and then end the program.

```
170 END
```

The complete program is

```
100 DEF FNR(X) = INT(X*100+.5)/100
110 PRINT "LABEL PRICE";
120 INPUT Z
130 PRINT "10% DISCOUNT IS";FNR(.9*Z)
140 PRINT "15% DISCOUNT IS";FNR(.85*Z)
150 PRINT "20% DISCOUNT IS";FNR(.8*Z)
160 GOTO 110
170 END
```

In lines 130, 140, and 150 the defined function is used. For a 10 percent discount, the selling price is 90 percent of the original price Z. Hence, we print out FNR(0.9*Z), which rounds off the value to the nearest cent as desired. Note the economy of using the defined function rather that writing out the expression in line 100 each time we want to print out a rounded dollar amount.

Example 2 - Carpet Estimating

We want to write a program that uses a subroutine to compute the price of installed carpet. Suppose that there are four grades of carpet and each is discounted as the quantity of carpet ordered increases. We will assume that the price structure is as follows:

		1	2	3
Grade	A	$10.00	$ 8.50	$ 7.25
	B	13.25	12.00	9.75
	C	16.00	14.00	11.25
	D	20.00	17.20	15.25

1. First 15 square yards
2. Any part of the order exceeding 15 but not more than 25 square yards
3. Anything over 25 square yards

When executed, the program should produce the following output:

```
HOW MANY ROOMS? (You type in)
FOR EACH ROOM, TYPE IN LENGTH
AND WIDTH IN FEET SEPARATED
BY A COMMA

ROOM                DIMENSIONS

1                    (You type in)
2                    (You type in)

    (Loop until all rooms are entered)

(Computer types out number) SQUARE YARDS REQUIRED
CARPET GRADE                COST OF ORDER
A                  (Computer types out,etc.)
B
C
D
```

Before getting involved in the program, we should think a bit about the output. Since the output is in dollars and cents, we may as well use the defined function from Example 1 to take care of rounding off the answers properly. So let's begin the program with that defined function.

```
100 DEF FNR(X) = INT(X*100+.5)/100
```

The next few lines follow without difficulty.

```
110 PRINT "HOW MANY ROOMS";
120 INPUT N
130 PRINT "FOR EACH ROOM, TYPE IN LENGTH"
140 PRINT "AND WIDTH IN FEET SEPARATED"
150 PRINT "BY A COMMA"
160 PRINT
170 PRINT "ROOM","DIMENSIONS"
180 PRINT
```

Now we are ready to call for the input of the room dimensions. We will use the variable A to keep track of the area of the rooms. Remember that the area of a room is its length times its width.

```
190 LET A = 0
200 FOR I = 1 TO N
210 PRINT I,
220 INPUT L,W
230 LET A = A+L*W
240 NEXT I
```

Since the total room area is now in square feet, we must divide this by 9 to convert to square yards, and then we will print out the quantity of carpet required.

```
250 LET A = A/9
260 PRINT A;"SQUARE YARDS REQUIRED"
```

At this point we may as well include the price table in the program in the form of DATA statements.

```
270 DATA 10,8.5,7.25
280 DATA 13.25,12,9.75
290 DATA 16,14,11.25
300 DATA 20,17.2,15.25
```

Next we can print out the heading required for the price printout.

```
310 PRINT
320 PRINT "CARPET GRADE","COST OF ORDER"
330 PRINT
```

Now we come to the point in the program where the subroutine will be useful. Since we don't know precisely where the subroutine should begin, we will simply use a large line number and correct it later if needed.

```
340 REM COMPUTE PRICE FOR GRADE A
350 GOSUB 800
```

Let's write the subroutine now. First, for each of the grades of carpet we need the three prices. We can do this by reading them from the DATA statements.

```
800 REM SUBROUTINE TO COMPUTE CARPET PRICE
810 READ C1,C2,C3
```

Next check to see if the area of the carpet is less than 15, between 15 and 25, or more than 25 square yards and then compute the price accordingly.

```
820 IF A > 25 THEN 860
830 IF A > 15 THEN 880
840 LET P = C1*A
850 GOTO 890
860 LET P = 15*C1 + 10*C2 + (A-25)*C3
870 GOTO 890
880 LET P = 15*C1 + (A-15)*C2
890 RETURN
```

Study this program segment to convince yourself that the price is being computed correctly. Now we can return to the main program and print out the first price.

```
360 PRINT "A",FNR(P)
```

Once this pattern has been established, the rest of the main program follows easily.

```
370 REM COMPUTE PRICE FOR GRADE B
380 GOSUB 800
390 PRINT "B",FNR(P)
400 REM COMPUTE PRICE FOR GRADE C
410 GOSUB 800
420 PRINT "C",FNR(P)
430 REM COMPUTE PRICE FOR GRADE D
440 GOSUB 800
450 PRINT "D",FNR(P)
460 END
```

The END statement in line 460 is needed to prevent the program from falling into the subroutine. The value of the subroutine becomes clear when we see that had it not been available, each of the four GOSUB statements would have had to be replaced with as many statements as in the subroutine.

The complete program is

```
100 DEF FNR(X) = INT(X*100+.5)/100
110 PRINT "HOW MANY ROOMS"
120 INPUT N
130 PRINT "FOR EACH ROOM, TYPE IN LENGTH"
140 PRINT "AND WIDTH IN FEET SEPARATED"
150 PRINT "BY A COMMA"
160 PRINT
170 PRINT "ROOM","DIMENSIONS"
180 PRINT
190 LET A = 0
200 FOR I = 1 TO N
210 PRINT I,
220 INPUT L,W
230 LET A = A+L*W
240 NEXT I
250 LET A = A/9
260 PRINT A;"SQUARE YARDS REQUIRED"
270 DATA 10,8.5,7.25
280 DATA 13.25,12,9.75
290 DATA 16,14,11.25
300 DATA 20,17.2,15.25
310 PRINT
320 PRINT "CARPET GRADE","COST OF ORDER"
330 PRINT
340 REM COMPUTE PRICE FOR GRADE A
350 GOSUB 800
360 PRINT "A",FNR(P)
370 REM COMPUTE PRICE FOR GRADE B
380 GOSUB 800
390 PRINT "B",FNR(P)
400 REM COMPUTE PRICE FOR GRADE C
410 GOSUB 800
420 PRINT "C",FNR(P)
430 REM COMPUTE PRICE FOR GRADE D
440 GOSUB 800
450 PRINT "D",FNR(P)
460 END
800 REM SUBROUTINE TO COMPUTE CARPET PRICE
```

```
810 READ C1,C2,C3
820 IF A > 25 THEN 860
830 IF A > 15 THEN 880
840 LET P = C1*A
850 GOTO 890
860 LET P = 15*C1 + 10*C2 + (A-25)*C3
870 GOTO 890
880 LET P = 15*C1 + (A-15)*C2
890 RETURN
```

Example 3 - Designing a House

This is an example on subroutines in a program using the graphics and color statements we used in Chapter 4. Your IBM Personal Computer must be equipped with the Color/Graphics Display Adapter. (See Appendix A.) As you read this program example, pay close attention to the REMARKS. The following statements are needed at the beginning of the program.

```
SCREEN 1,0
COLOR 1,1
```

to enter graphics mode with color.

The program draws a house. The roof is drawn first and the designer is asked to decide on whether the roof will contain windows and whether it should be painted. The selection of the window position and what regions are to be painted is done with the POINT program you used in Chapter 7. The placement of the window is done by moving the point to the position you wish using the L, R, U, and D keys on the keyboard. In order to paint a region. the point must be inside that region.

The frame is drawn next and decisions are made by the designer concerning windows, a door and painting. The program follows. Notice that the window drawing subroutine (line number 1000) and painting subroutine (line number 2000) use the POINT moving program (line number 4000) as a subroutine.

If you wish to enter and run this program, you may save yourself some typing by loading the POINT program you saved in Chapter 7 and renumbering it to begin at line 4000.

```
100 REM * DESIGNING A HOUSE *
110 SCREEN 1,0
120 COLOR 1,1
130 PRINT "ENTER SCALE FACTOR (1 TO 20).";
140 REM * THE SCALE FACTOR DETERMINES THE SIZE OF
145 REM THE HOUSE. IT SHOULD BE A NUMBER BETWEEN
150 REM 1 AND 20!  *
160 INPUT SCALE
170 CLS
180 DRAW "S = SCALE;"
190 LET ROOF$ = "L20 E20 F20 L20"
200 DRAW ROOF$
210 PRINT "WINDOW ?  (Y/N)";
220 INPUT W$
230 IF W$ = "Y" THEN GOSUB 1000
240 PRINT "PAINT ?  (Y/N)";
250 INPUT P$
260 IF P$ = "Y" THEN GOSUB 2000
270 PRINT A,B
280 LET FRAME$ = "L15 D20 R30 U20 L15"
290 DRAW FRAME$
300 PRINT "WINDOW ?  (Y/N)";
310 INPUT W$
320 IF W$ = "Y" THEN GOSUB 1000
330 PRINT "DOOR ?  (Y/N)";
340 INPUT D$
350 IF D$ = "Y" THEN GOSUB 3000
360 PRINT "PAINT ?  (Y/N)";
370 INPUT P$
380 IF P$ = "Y" THEN GOSUB 2000
390 END
1000 REM * THIS IS THE WINDOW DRAWING SUBROUTINE *
1010 GOSUB 4000
1020 LET WINDOW$ = "BU2 R2 D5 L4 U5 R2"
1030 DRAW WINDOW$
1035 DRAW "BM160,100"
1040 PRINT "WINDOW ?  (Y/N)";
1050 INPUT W$
1060 IF W$ = "Y" THEN GOSUB 1000
1070 RETURN
2000 REM * THIS IS THE PAINTING SUBROUTINE *
```

```
2010 GOSUB 4000
2015 PRESET(A,B)
2020 PAINT(A,B),3,3
2025 DRAW "BM160,100"
2030 RETURN
3000 REM * THIS IS THE DOOR DRAWING SUBROUTINE *
3010 LET MOVEDOOR$ = "BM-2,+20"
3015 PRINT A,B
3020 LET DOOR$ = "R4 U6 L4 D6"
3025 DRAW MOVEDOOR$ + DOOR$
3030 RETURN
4000 REM * THIS IS THE POINT MOVING SUBROUTINE *
4010 LET A = 160
4020 LET B = 100
4030 PRESET(A,B)
4040 PSET(A,B)
4050 LET A$ = INKEY$
4060 IF A$ = "D" THEN B = B+5
4070 IF A$ = "U" THEN B = B-5
4080 IF A$ = "L" THEN A = A-5
4090 IF A$ = "R" THEN A = A+5
4100 IF A$ = "Q" THEN 4120
4110 GOTO 4030
4120 LET A$ = ""
4130 PRINT A,B
4140 RETURN
```

Note: Be prepared for a problem when painting. If the scale factor is too big, and your typing goes into any part of the house that is drawn on the screen, it will break the boundary and the paint will cover most of the screen.

11–5 PROBLEMS

1. Study the program below and write down what will be printed out if the program is executed.

```
100 DEF FNA(X) = 2+X
110 DEF FNB(Y) = 10*Y
120 DEF FNC(Z) = Z^2
130 LET R = 2
```

```
140 LET S = 3
150 LET T = 5
160 PRINT FNC(T),FNA(S),FNB(R)
170 LET R = S+T
180 PRINT FNA(R) + FNB(S) + FNC(T)
190 END
```

2. What will be printed out if the program below is executed?

```
100 DEF FNX(A) = 6*A
110 DEF FNY(B) = B+10
120 DEF FNZ(C) = C^3
130 READ P,Q,R
140 DATA 1,2,3
150 PRINT FNX(R),FNZ(P),FNY(Q)
160 PRINT FNY(P+Q) + FNX(R)
170 END
```

3. The area of a circle is Pi times R squared, and the volume of a sphere is 4/3 times Pi times R cubed. Pi is 3.14159, and R is either the radius of the circle or the radius of the sphere. Define two DEF statements, one for the circle and one for the sphere. Set up a FOR NEXT loop on R for R from 1 to 10 in steps of 0.5. Use the defined functions to print out a table of areas and volumes for each of the values of R.

4. What will be output by the following program if it is executed?

```
100 DIM A(5)
110 FOR I = 1 TO 5
120 READ A(I)
130 NEXT I
140 DATA 6,2,7,1,3
150 GOSUB 500
160 LET A(3) = 10
170 GOSUB 500
180 LET A(5) = 8
190 GOSUB 500
200 END
500 FOR I = 1 TO 4
510 LET A(I) = A(I+1)
520 NEXT I
```

```
530 GOSUB 600
540 RETURN
600 FOR J = 1 TO 5
610 PRINT A(J),
620 NEXT J
630 RETURN
```

5. What will be printed out if the program below is executed?

```
100 LET X = 10
110 GOSUB 500
120 PRINT S
130 LET Z = X/2
140 GOSUB 500
150 PRINT S
160 LET X = X+3
170 GOSUB 500
180 PRINT S
190 END
500 LET S = 0
510 FOR Y = 1 TO X
520 LET S = S+Y
530 NEXT Y
540 RETURN
```

6. Assume that a one-dimensional array Z contains numbers to be added together. The first element of the array Z(1) gives the number of elements that follow in the array and are to be summed. Write a subroutine beginning in line 800 to compute the sum of the elements after Z(1). Assign the sum to the variable T. Terminate the subroutine with a RETURN statement. Assume that the array Z has been properly dimensioned and that the values in the array have been loaded in the main program.

7. X is a one-dimensional array. The first element of the array X(1) gives the number of pieces of data that follow in the array. Write a subroutine beginning in line 500 to search through that array for the largest value. Assign this value to the variable L. Terminate the subroutine with a RETURN statement. Assume that the array X has been properly dimensioned and loaded with numbers elsewhere.

8. Suppose that as part of a printout we need a series of seventy-two * characters in a straight line across the page. Write a subroutine beginning in line 1000 to do this. Terminate the subroutine with a RETURN statement.

9. Assume that a one-dimensional array Y is loaded with numbers. The first element Y(1) gives the number of elements to follow. We want a subroutine to calculate the mean (M) and standard deviation (S) of the numbers in the array which follow the first element. Begin the subroutine in line 900 and terminate with a RETURN statement. The formulas for calculation of the mean and standard deviation are given below.

$$\text{Mean} = (\text{Sum of values})/N$$

$$\text{Standard deviation} = \sqrt{\frac{N\times(\text{sum of squares of values}) - (\text{sum of values})^2}{N\times(N-1)}}$$

11–6 PRACTICE TEST

Check your progress with the following practice test. The answers are given at the end of the book.

1. If DEF FNA(X) = SQR(X)+3*X, Z = 2.5, and W = 10, what is

   a. FNA(1)

   b. FNA(4)

   c. FNA(9)

   d. FNA(Z*W)

2. What will be printed out if we execute the following program?

```
100 DEF FNR(X) = X*X
110 DEF FNS(X) = 3*X
120 DEF FNT(Y) = Y+1
130 LET A = 1
140 PRINT FNT(A),FNR(A);FNS(A)
150 LET M = 4
160 PRINT FNR(SQR(M))
170 END
```

3. With regards to subroutines

   a. How do you pass control from the main program to the subroutine?

   b. How do you pass control from the subroutine back to the main program?

4. What will be printed out if we execute the following program?

```
100 LET A = 1
110 GOSUB 200
120 LET A = A+4
130 GOSUB 200
140 LET A = A-2
150 GOSUB 200
160 END
200 REM SUBROUTINE
210 IF A < 2 THEN 250
220 IF A = 3 THEN 270
230 PRINT "RED"
240 GOTO 280
250 PRINT "WHITE"
260 GOTO 280
270 PRINT "BLUE"
280 RETURN
```

CHAPTER 12

RANDOM NUMBERS AND SIMULATIONS

12–1 OBJECTIVES

One of the most interesting applications of computers concerns simulation of events or processes that involve an element of chance. Examples might be using the computer to simulate gambling games or perhaps investigating the number of bank tellers required to ensure that arriving customers do not have to wait more than a few minutes to be served. In this chapter we will see how the computer can be used to handle problems of this type. Our objectives are as follows.

Characteristics of Random-Number Generators

Your IBM Personal Computer has a random-number generator function that is the heart of all programs involving the element of chance, or randomness. We will learn how these random-number generators can be employed in BASIC programs.

Random Numbers with Special Characteristics

Generally, the random-number generator is used to produce sets of random numbers with characteristics specified by the programmer. We will see how this is done and how any desired set of numbers can be generated.

Programming and Simulations

The programming exercises and problems in this chapter will use simulations and applications that involve the element of chance.

12–2 DISCOVERY EXERCISES

Setting Up The Random-Number Generator

Before beginning the computer work, we must discuss some important characteristics of random-number generators. By their very nature, these generators produce sequences of numbers that appear to have no pattern or relationship. For a random-number generator to be useful, each time we execute a program that utilizes it we should get a different sequence of numbers. However, this gives rise to an interesting question. Suppose a program that uses random numbers is not working correctly. If the problem is connected with the random numbers it might be extrememly difficult to correct since different random numbers are generated each time the program is executed. Consequently, provisions are always included so that a sequence of random numbers can be repeated each time the program is executed. Remember, though, that this feature of BASIC should be used only when you are trouble-shooting a program.

Computer Work

1. Turn on the computer and bring up BASICA. Unless otherwise specified, assume that different sequences of numbers are to be generated each time a program is executed.

2. Enter the following program:

```
90 RANDOMIZE
100 FOR I = 1 TO 9
110 PRINT RND
120 NEXT I
130 END
```

Execute the program and when the random number seed is requested, type in any number between -32768 and 32767. Then record the largest and smallest numbers that were printed out.

____

3. Execute the program again and give a different value for the seed. Did the same numbers appear?

____

What was the largest number typed out?

____

What was the smallest number?

____

4. Deactivate the RANDOMIZE statement by editing line 90 as follows.

```
90 REM RANDOMIZE
```

Run the program several times. What happened?

____

EDIT line 110 as follows.

```
110 PRINT RND(0)
```

Run the program. Are different random numbers printed out?

____

5. Display the program in memory. Reactivate the RANDOMIZE statement by editing out REM in line 90 as follows.

```
90 RANDOMIZE
```

Once again the random-number generator can now be seeded each time the program is executed. Run the program several times. Does RANDOMIZE change the value printed by RND(0)?

____

EDIT line 110 as follows.

```
110 PRINT RND(1)
```

Run the program. How does this program output compare with the program output you recorded in Step 2 where line 110 was

```
110 PRINT RND
```

6. Clear out the program in memory and type in the following program.

```
60 LET Y$ = TIME$
70 LET A$ = MID$(Y$,7,2)
80 LET N = VAL(A$)
90 PRINT N,Y$
100 END
```

Run the program several times and record the values of N that are printed out.

These numbers represent the seconds on the internal clock of the IBM Personal Computer. The TIME$ string is the time on the clock and is represented using eight characters as hh:mm:ss where hh is the hour, mm is the minutes and ss is the seconds. Y$ is set equal to TIME$ to retrieve the time and, as you may recall, MID$(Y$,7,2) picks out 2 characters from the string Y$ starting at character 7, which is the number of seconds on the clock at that time. This string, representing the seconds, is then assigned to A$ and then converted to a number with the assignment N = VAL(A$). This will be the proceedure used to seed the RANDOMIZE statement in the remaining programs in this chapter and will relieve us from having to give a seed everytime the program is run.

. Clear out the program in memory. We will use the clock in the IBM Personal Computer to select the seed (N) for the RANDOMIZE statement in line 90 of the following examples. Enter the following program:

```
60 LET Y$ = TIME$
70 LET A$ = MID$(Y$,7,2)
80 LET N = VAL(A$)
90 RANDOMIZE(N)
100 LET L = .5
110 LET S = .5
120 FOR I = 1 TO 100
130 LET X = RND
140 IF X > L THEN 170
150 IF X < S THEN 190
160 GOTO 200
170 LET L = X
180 GOTO 200
190 LET S = X
200 NEXT I
210 PRINT "LARGEST = ";L
220 PRINT "SMALLEST = 2"S
230 END
```

This program examines all the numbers generated by the RND function and keeps track of the largest and smallest numbers generated. As the program stands, it will generate 100 random numbers. Execute the program and record what was typed out.

. Type

```
120 FOR I = 1 TO 1000
```

Now the program will generate 1000 random numbers. Execute the program and record what was printed out.

Based upon what you have seen thus far, what do you believe is the largest number that will be generated by the RND function?

____

What about the smallest?

____

9. Now let's go on to some other ideas associated with random numbers. Clear out the program in memory space and enter the following program:

```
60 LET Y$ = TIME$
70 LET A$ = MID$(Y$,7,2)
80 LET N = VAL(A$)
90 RANDOMIZE(N)
100 FOR I = 1 TO 10
110 PRINT INT(2*RND)
120 NEXT I
130 END
```

Execute the program and record the output.

____

What were the only two numbers typed out?

____

10. Type

```
110 PRINT INT(3*RND)
```

Display the program. If this program is executed, what numbers do you think will be typed out?

____

Can you predict anything about the sequence or pattern in which the numbers will be typed out?

____

1. Type

```
110 PRINT INT(2*RND+1)
```

What do you think the program will do now?

____

Execute the program and record the output.

____

2. Type

```
110 PRINT INT(4*RND+4)
```

If the program is executed, what do you think will be printed out?

____

Execute the program and describe the output.

____

Any pattern to the output?

____

3. Type

```
110 PRINT INT(30*RND)/10
```

Display the program and study it carefully. What do you think this program will print out?

____

Execute the program and describe the printout.

____

14. Type

```
100 PRINT INT(200*RND)/100
```

Display the program in memory. What do you think will happen if this program is executed?

____

See if you were right. Execute the program and record the output below.

____

15. Turn off the computer. This terminates the computer work for now.

12–3 DISCUSSION

Now that you have seen some of the characteristics of the random-number generator on the computer, we can profitably proceed to a complete discussion of the matter.

■ **RND function generates numbers in the range 0 to 0.9999999.**

Random-Number Generators

We will not become involved with the details of how random numbers are generated. It is enough to say that there are several mathematical methods to produce these numbers. The random-number generator is called on with the RND function. This function is used like the other built-in functions in BASIC that were studied previously, but differs in two important respects.

Recall that the argument of a function (what the function works on) determines the result. Thus, SQR(4) is 2, INT(3.456) is 3, and so forth. The RND function does not require an argument. This is the first difference. If used, the effect of the argument of the RND function depends only upon whether the argument is negative, positve or zero. Negative arguments of the RND function (and the RANDOMIZE function) cause the random-number generator to be (re)seeded and are discussed in detail in the *BASIC* reference manual.

Positive arguments act as though no argument was used. Zero as an argument will cause the same random number to be repeated. If we wish to have the same set of numbers repeated, we would REMark out or delete the RANDOMIZE or seeding statement from the program. Defined variables may also be used as arguments of the RND function.

The second major difference is that there seems to be no pattern or rule used in generating numbers with the RND function. Of course, this is precisely the point of the function. RND stands for "random." The function generates numbers between 0 and 1 at random. All the numbers in the interval have an equal chance of showing up. Actually, the range of numbers generated is from 0.0000000 to 0.9999999. Zero can show up occasionally, but the number 1 never occurs.

Automatic Seeding of the Random-Number Generator

The program lines

```
60 LET Y$ = TIME$
70 LET A$ = MID$(Y$,7,2)
80 LET N = VAL(A$)
90 RANDOMIZE(N)
```

can be used to automatically seed the random-number generator each time a program is executed. As previously described, this "subroutine" uses the seconds on the IBM Personal Computer clock as the seed. These lines provide at most 60 different seeds. You might consider ways to increase the number of possible seeds using this same basic idea.

Designing Sets of Random Numbers

Most often we do not want random numbers in the range produced by the RND function. We might want random integers (whole numbers) over a certain range or a set of random numbers with a particular set of characteristics. Therefore, we must give some thought to how to generate sets of random numbers with characteristics we can specify.

Let's begin with the characteristics of the RND function. RND delivers numbers in the range 0 to 1, that is, from 0 to slightly less than 1. If we multiply RND by N, we multiply the range of the function by N. Thus, N*RND will produce random numbers in the range 0 to N. If desired, we could shift the numbers (keeping the same range) by adding a number. N*RND+A would produce random numbers over the range A to (A+N) or from A to slightly less than (A+N). Finally, if desired, we could take the integer part of an expression, using the INT function, to produce random integers. The examples below indicate how the RND function might be used.

BASIC Expression	Result
5*RND + 10	Random numbers in the range 10 to 15
INT(5*RND + 10)	Random integers 10, 11, 12, 13, 14
INT(2*RND + 1)	Random integers 1, 2
100*RND	Random numbers in the range 0 to 100

In your studies you may have encountered the notion of mean and standard deviation (see problem 9 in Chapter 11). We can use the RND function to generate numbers that appear to be drawn from a collection of numbers having a given mean and standard deviation. The rule for generating these numbers is

$$X = M+S((\textit{sum of 12 numbers from RND function}) - 6)$$

where M and S are the desired mean and standard deviation, respectively. This is an application in which a subroutine would be very useful. As defined above, the values of X will appear to be coming from a collection of numbers with mean M and standard deviation S. The values of X can be used to simulate a process following the bell curve that you have probably seen in textbooks.

Troubleshooting Programs that Use Random Numbers

We have already pointed out that BASIC provides a way to execute a program several times and repeat the sequence of random numbers that are generated by the RND function. It is usually wise to write programs initially so that they do generate the same sequence of random numbers each time they are executed. Once you are sure that the program is working correctly, you can modify the program to produce the randomness that is the central idea in the RND function.

12—4 PROGRAM EXAMPLES

Now we will go through several examples to illustrate how random numbers can be used. Study these examples carefully and make sure you understand exactly what is taking place.

Example 1 - Flipping Coins

One of the easiest applications of random numbers is a coin-tossing simulation. We want to write a program that when executed will produce the following printout:

```
TOSS        OUTCOME
1           H
2           T
3           T
4           H
     etc.
```

The outcome is to be determined randomly for each toss of the coin, with both heads and tails having equal probability. The program should print out the results of ten coin tosses.

The first part of the program generates the heading and the space indicated in the printout above.

```
100 PRINT "TOSS","OUTCOME"
110 PRINT
```

Now we must open the loop to generate the ten tosses of the coin.

```
120 FOR I = 1 TO 10
```

The next step is to generate 0s and 1s randomly. We will assume that the occurrence of a 0 means a "head" and the occurrence of a 1 means a "tail." You should be able to convince yourself that the following statement will produce 0s and 1s randomly.

```
130 LET X = INT(2*RND)
```

Now we analyze X to see whether a head (0) or a tail (1) has occurred.

```
140 IF X = 0 THEN 170
150 PRINT I,"T"
160 GOTO 180
170 PRINT I,"H"
180 NEXT I
```

All that remains now is the END statement.

```
190 END
```

The complete program, including seeding, is listed below.

```
60 LET Y$ = TIME$
70 LET A$ = MID$(Y$,7,2)
80 LET N = VAL(A$)
90 RANDOMIZE(N)
100 PRINT "TOSS","OUTCOME"
110 PRINT
120 FOR I = 1 TO 10
130 LET X = INT(2*RND)
140 IF X = 0 THEN 170
150 PRINT I,"T"
160 GOTO 180
170 PRINT I,"H"
180 NEXT I
190 END
```

This is a good program for demonstrating how the computer can be instructed to produce either different sequences of random numbers or identical sequences each time the program is executed. Make the necessary changes in the program to see this work.

Example 2 - Random Integers

The next problem is to write a BASIC program to generate and print out fifty random integers (whole numbers) over the range 10 to 15. The only part of the program that will require much thought is the statement to generate the random integers, so we will concentrate on this one statement.

Remember that RND generates numbers over the range 0 to 1. Thus, 6*RND will generate numbers in the range 0 to 6. Actually the upper limit is 5.999999. By using the integer function we can convert from random numbers to random integers. INT(6*RND) will produce the integers 0, 1, 2, 3, 4, 5 randomly. Now it is clear that to get the desired numbers, we must add 10. Thus, the expression INT(6*RND) + 10 will produce the numbers we want.

Once we have this one line figured out, the program follows easily.

```
100 FOR I = 1 TO 50
110 LET Y = INT(6*RND) + 10
120 PRINT Y,
130 NEXT I
140 END
```

Example 3 - Distribution of Random Numbers

Suppose we generate a great number of integers at random over the range 1 to 10. If the random-number generator on the computer is working the way it should, we would expect to get the same number of each of the integers. If we generated 10,000 integers, we would expect to get 1000 1s, 1000 2s, and so on. Our problem will be to write a BASIC program to do a tally of the random integers as they are generated and then print out the totals. Inspection of these totals will tell us how good the random-number generator on the computer really is.

First let's think about how we are going to do the tally. A good way to do this is to use a one-dimensional subscripted array. X(1) will contain the number of 1s generated, X(2) the number of 2s, and so forth on up to X(10). Thus, the first task is to dimension the array and set all the values in the array equal to 0.

```
100 DIM X(10)
110 FOR I = 1 TO 10
120 X(I) = 0
130 NEXT I
```

Next we open a loop to generate 10,000 numbers, generate the random integers, then use the integers as subscripts to increment the appropriate counters in the array.

```
140 FOR I = 1 TO 10000
150 LET Y = INT(10*RND) + 1
160 LET X(Y) = X(Y) + 1
170 NEXT I
```

Now all that remains is to print out the contents of the array X.

```
180 FOR J = 1 TO 10
190 PRINT J,X(J)
200 NEXT J
210 END
```

The complete program, including seeding, follows:

```
60 LET Y$ = TIME$
70 LET A$ = MID$(Y$,7,2)
80 LET N = VAL(A$)
90 RANDOMIZE(N)
100 DIM X(10)
110 FOR I = 1 TO 10
120 X(I) = 0
130 NEXT I
140 FOR I = 1 TO 10000
150 LET Y = INT(10*RND) + 1
160 LET X(Y) = X(Y) + 1
170 NEXT I
180 FOR J = 1 TO 10
190 PRINT J,X(J)
200 NEXT J
210 END
```

It might be interesting for you to execute this program and see for yourself how the random-number generator checks out. If you decrease the number of integers generated, the agreement between what you expect and what actually takes place should get worse. On the other hand, if you generate more random numbers, the agreement should get better.

Example 4 - Random Walk

This program will simulate a random walk on the display screen using the graphics mode. Your IBM Personal Computer will require the Color/Graphics Display Adapter to run this program.

If you walk about in a city aimlessly, or at random, you are performing a random walk. There will be many different random walks or paths in a city.

The program below simulates a random walk in a city where all the blocks have the same size (10). Lines 30 and 40 clear the screen and place the computer in graphics mode. Line 80 allows you to establish the seed for the random number generator. Line 100 randomly assigns the values 1, 2, 3, and 4 to the variable called WHICHWAY. Lines 110 through 500 use WHICHWAY to determine which way to go on the next part of the random walk.

```
20 REM *** RANDOM WALK ***
30 CLS
40 SCREEN 1,0
50 LET Y$ = TIME$
60 LET A$ = MID$(Y$,7,2)
70 LET N = VAL(A$)
80 RANDOMIZE(N)
90 FOR I = 1 TO 500
100 LET WHICHWAY = INT(4*RND) + 1
110 ON WHICHWAY GOSUB 200,300,400,500
120 NEXT I
130 END
200 DRAW "L10"
210 RETURN
300 DRAW "R10"
310 RETURN
400 DRAW "U10"
410 RETURN
500 DRAW "D10"
510 RETURN
```

Example 5 - Birthday Pairs in a Crowd

Suppose that fifty strangers get together in a room. What is the probability that two of the people have the same birthday? We consider only the day of the year, not the year of birth. This problem is a famous one in probability theory and has surprising results. We can attack the problem with the following strategy. By generating random integers over the range 1 to 365, we can simulate a birthday for each of the strangers. If we use a one-dimensional array for the birthdays as they are generated, it is easy to check for identical birthdays. Beginning with the first birthday B(1), we check to see if it matches any of the remaining ones. Then we do the same thing for B(2), and so on.

For this example, we will depart from the usual method and will look at the complete program, then go back and explain what is taking place in each line.

```
60 LET Y$ = TIME$
70 LET A$ = MID$(Y$,7,2)
80 LET N = VAL(A$)
90 RANDOMIZE(N)
100 DIM B(50)
110 FOR I = 1 TO 50
120 LET B(I) = INT(365*RND) + 1
130 NEXT I
140 LET F = 0
150 FOR I = 1 TO 49
160 FOR J = I+1 TO 50
170 IF B(I) <> B(J) THEN 190
180 LET F = F+1
190 NEXT J
200 NEXT I
210 PRINT "NUMBER OF BIRTHDAY PAIRS IS";F
220 END
```

Of course, line 100 merely dimensions an array for fifty elements. Lines 110 through 130 load the array with random integers selected over the range 1 to 365 inclusive. In line 140, we set the variable F equal to 0. We will use this variable to keep track of the number of birthdays that will be compared with the rest of the birthdays in the list. Since there must be at least one birthday left in the list to compare with, the value of I stops at 49. In line 160, the second half of the comparison is set up.

J begins at the next value past the current value of I and runs through the rest of the list. The test for a birthday pair is made in line 170. If no match if found, we jump to the next value of J. If a match is found, the pair counter is increased by 1 in line 180. The results are printed out in line 210. One problem with the program is that it would record three people having the same birthday as two birthday pairs. Can you figure out a way to fix this?

This is a very interesting program to experiment with. The number of the people in the crowd can be modified with simple changes in the program. The program can be executed many times to see how many birthday pairs on the average will be found in a crowd of a specified size.

12–5 PROBLEMS

. Write a program to generate and print out twenty-five random numbers of the form X.Y where X and Y are digits selected randomly from the set 0, 1 , 2 ,3 . . . 9.

. Write a program to generate and print out fifty integers selected at random from the range 13 to 25.

. What will be printed out if the following program is executed?

```
60 LET Y$ = TIME$
70 LET A$ = MID$(Y$,7,2)
80 LET N = VAL(A$)
90 RANDOMIZE(N)
100 FOR N = 1 TO 20
110 PRINT INT(20*RND+1)/100
120 NEXT N
130 END
```

. If the following program is executed, what will be printed out?

```
60 LET Y$ = TIME$
70 LET A$ = MID$(Y$,7,2)
80 LET N = VAL(A$)
90 RANDOMIZE(N)
100 FOR I = 1 TO 10
110 PRINT INT(100*RND)/10
120 NEXT I
130 END
```

. Write a program that will simulate tossing a coin, 10, 50, 500, and 1000 times. In each case, print out the total number of heads and tails that occur.

6. Construct a dice-throwing simulation in BASIC. The dice are to be thrown twenty times. For each toss, print out the dice faces that are uppermost.

7. Write a program to generate and print out the average of 100 random numbers selected from the range 0 to 1.

8. Modify the program of Example 5 and execute it as many times as needed to find the size of crowd such that there is a 50 percent chance that at least two people in the crowd have the same birthday.

9. John and Bill want to meet at the library. Each agrees to arrive at the library sometime between 1 and 2 P.M. They further agree that they will wait 10 minutes after arriving (but not after 2 P.M.), and if the other person has not arrived, will leave. Write a BASIC program to compute the probability that John and Bill will meet one another. Do a simulation of the problem using the random-number generator.

10. Suppose a basket contains colored golf balls. There are ten red balls, five blue, two green, and eleven yellow. Write a BASIC program to simulate drawing five balls at random from the bucket if they are not replaced after being drawn in sequence.

11. Use the rule given in the discussion section in this chapter to generate and print out twenty-five numbers selected at random from a bell curve distribution of numbers with mean 10 and standard deviation 2. Round off the numbers to two places past the decimal point.

12. Suppose a soap manufacturer decides to select a five character brand name. The first, third, and fifth characters are selected at random from the letters BCDFGHJKLMNPQRSTVWXYZ. The second and fourth letters are selected at random from the vowels AEIOU. Write a program to generate and print out one hundred trial soap names using the rules above.

13. Modify the program from problem 6 to simulate tossing a pair of dice 1000 times. Print out the number of times each of the eleven possible outcomes happened in the simulation.

12–6 PRACTICE TEST

Take the following test to see how you are progressing. The answers are given at the end of the book.

Write a BASIC program to generate and print out 100 random integers selected from the set 1, 2, 3, and 4.

Write a BASIC program to generate and print out 100 random numbers over the range 25 to 50.

What will be printed out if we execute the following program?

```
60 LET Y$ = TIME$
70 LET A$ = MID$(Y$,7,2)
80 LET N = VAL(A$)
90 RANDOMIZE(N)
100 FOR I = 1 TO 10
110 LET N = INT(2*RND+1)
120 IF N = 1 THEN 150
130 PRINT "WHITE"
140 GOTO 160
150 PRINT "RED"
160 NEXT I
170 END
```

What will be printed out if we execute the following program?

```
60 LET Y$ = TIME$
70 LET A$ = MID$(Y$,7,2)
80 LET N = VAL(A$)
90 RANDOMIZE(N)
100 FOR J = 1 TO 5
110 PRINT INT(1000*RND)/100
120 NEXT J
130 END
```

APPENDIX A

DUAL MONOCHROME AND COLOR ADAPTER

The graphics mode is not available when your IBM Personal Computer is using the Monochrome Display and Printer Adapter for screen display. If, in addition to the Monochrome Adapter, your IBM Personal Computer is also equipped with a Color/Graphics Monitor Adapter, then the graphics mode is available after the program below is run to switch to the Color/Graphics Monitor Adapter for screen display. Of course, you will need to connect a color or black and white monitor or TV set to the Color/Graphics Monitor Adapter and turn it on.

Type in the following program.

```
10 REM GRAPHICS
20 REM A PROGRAM TO SWITCH TO THE
30 REM COLOR/GRAPHICS MONITOR ADAPTER
40 KEY OFF
50 CLS
60 WIDTH 80
70 DEF SEG=0
80 LET A = PEEK(&H410)
90 POKE &H140,(A AND &HCF) OR &H20
100 WIDTH 40
110 SCREEN 1
120 SCREEN 0
130 LOCATE ,,1,6,7
140 END
```

Instruction for formatting a diskette may be found in Steps 11 through 13 of the Discovery Exercises in Chapter 5. Save this program for later use on a formatted diskette with the name GRAPHICS by typing in

```
SAVE"GRAPHICS <ENTER>
```

Run the program. Notice that your IBM Display Monitor goes dark and **OK** appears on the color or black and white TV/monitor you have connected to the Color/Graphics Monitor Adapter.

In order to place the Personal Computer in graphics mode, you must enter the statement SCREEN 1,0. This statements sets the medium resolution graphics mode and permits the use of color.

To run the program GRAPHICS once it has been saved to diskette type in

```
RUN"GRAPHICS <ENTER>
```

This command will switch the Personal Computer the Color/Graphics Adapter. You will still need to enter the statement SCREEN 1,0 to set the medium resolution graphics mode.

In order to switch back to the Monochrome Display and Printer Adapter, you should run the following program. You may wish to save this program as MONO on a formatted disk for later use.

```
10 REM MONO
20 REM A PROGRAM TO SWITCH TO A
30 REM MONOCHROME DISPLAY AND PRINTER ADAPTER
30 KEY OFF
40 CLS
50 WIDTH 40
60 DEF SEG=0
70 A=PEEK(&H410)
80 POKE &H410,A OR &H30
90 WIDTH 80
100 LOCATE ,,1,12,13
110 KEY ON
120 END
```

In order to run the mono program that has been saved on diskette, type in

```
RUN"MONO <ENTER>
```

These two programs allow you to switch back and forth between the IBM Monochrome Display and a standard TV monitor or televison set.

APPENDIX B

GLOSSARY

ABS(X) A BASIC function that takes the absolute value of X. Positive values of X remain positive. Negative values of X become positive.

Arithmetic Operators Addition +, subtraction –, multiplication *, division /, and exponention ^.

ASC(A$) A BASIC function that converts the first character in A$ to its equivalent position number in the ASCII character set.

AUTO A command for automatically numbering lines of a BASIC program.

BASIC An acronynm for "Beginners All-Purpose Instruction Code". More people know how to program computers in BASIC than any other language.

CHR$(N) A BASIC function that returns the Nth character from the ASCII character set.

CIRCLE A graphics mode statement that draws a circle with a specified center and radius.

CLS A statement that clears the screen.

COLOR A graphics mode statement that set one of the 16 background colors and sets one of the two palettes used by the DRAW, CIRCLE, PAINT, and PSET commands.

Control Characters These are characters typed on the keyboard while holding down the Ctrl key. They are used to send special signals to the computer.

DATA A statement used to hold information within a program. This information is called for with the READ statement.

DEF A statement used to define functions which are lengthy and will be used often in a program.

Deleting BASIC Statements Type the line number of the statement to be deleted and then press ENTER.

DIM A statement used to specify the size and reserve space for arrays.

Double Subscripts Indicated within parentheses following a variable name, and separated by a comma. Used to specify a row and column number in an array. A(3,5), for example, means the element in the two dimensional array A at row 3 and column 5.

DRAW A graphics mode statement that draws line segments using the graphics sublanguage commands. It allows you to draw pictures.

EDIT A command that displays the line specified which can then be modified.

END Marks the end of a BASIC program or the end of the main program.

E Notation A notation used in BASIC to express either very large or very small numbers.

FILES A command that lists the files on a diskette

FOR NEXT Statements used in BASIC to set up loops.

GOSUB A statement used to transfer program control to a subroutine.

GOTO An unconditional branch statement.

INKEY$ A BASIC function that allows the program to read a character from the keyboard.

INPUT A statement that calls for input of information from the keyboard.

Inserting BASIC Statements Type in the statement using a line number not already in use.

IF THEN A conditional branch statement.

IF THEN ELSE A conditional branch statement.

INT(X) A BASIC function that takes the integer part of X. The integer part of X is defined as the first integer less than or equal to X.

KEY A statement that allows us to store a string in one of the keys F1 through F10. Thus, KEY 7, "RENUM" would store the word RENUM in key F7 and would display RENUM on the screen when F7 is pressed.

KILL A command that erases a file on a diskette. For example, KILL AVERAGE will erase the file called AVERAGE from the diskette in drive A.

LEN(A$) A BASIC function used to determine the length of a string in characters. For example, if A$ = "HOUSE" then LEN(A$) is 5.

LET Identifies an assignment statement. It is always followed by a variable name, an equal sign, and a BASIC expression. The LET in the assignment statement is optional.

LIST A command used to tell the computer to print out the program in memory.

LOAD A command that loads a file from a diskette to the computer memory.

**MID$** A statement that returns the requested part of a given string. For example, if A$ = "together", then MID$(A$,5,3) will return the string "the".

NEW A command that erases the current program in memory.

Numeric Variable Names The IBM Personal Computer allows variable names up to 40 characters long. The first character must be a letter.

PAINT A graphics mode statement that colors in an area bounded by a specified color starting at a specified point in a given color.

PALETTE One of two sets of colors which are used by graphics mode commands.

PLAY A statement that plays notes written in the music sublanguage.

PRINT A statement that sends information from the computer to the screen.

PSET A graphics mode statement that sets a point at a specified position on the screen.

Random Numbers A sequence of numbers generated by the RND function. They appear to have no pattern or relationship to one another.

READ A statement that calls for input of information stored in DATA statements within the program.

RENUM A command that renumbers the program in memory.

Replacing BASIC Statements Retype the statement to be replaced including the line number.

RETURN A statement used to transfer program control back from a subroutine to the main program.

RANDOMIZE A statement used to reseed the random number generator.

RND A BASIC function used to generate random numbers.

RUN A command used to tell the computer to begin execution of the program in memory.

SAVE A command that saves a file from memory to diskette. For example, SAVE AVERAGE would save the program currently in memory to the diskette in drive A under the name AVERAGE.

SCREEN A statement that sets one of three screen modes for the IBM Personal Computer.

SGN(X) A BASIC function that determines the sign of X. SGN(X) is +1, 0, -1 as X is positive, zero, or negative respectively.

Single Subscripts Indicated within parentheses following a variable name. Used to specify a particular element in an array. A(6), for example, means the sixth element of the one dimensional array A.

SQR(X) A BASIC function that takes the square root of X. X cannot be negative.

String Variable Names BASIC string variable names are allowed to be up to 40 characters long. They must start with a letter and end with a $ sign.

SYSTEM A command that ends the BASIC mode, closes all files, and returns to DOS.

TAB A BASIC function that will tab to a specific position when in a PRINT statement.

TROFF A command that turns off the trace mode.

TRON A command that turns on the trace mode which prints each line number of the program as it is executed. It helps in debugging a program.

PRACTICE TEST SOLUTIONS

Chapter 2

1. Press the ENTER key.

2. Press the following three keys. While holding down the key marked Ctrl, press the Alt key and then the Del key.

3. *

4. Type CLS and press the ENTER key.

5. Division.

6. The number 2 will be displayed on the screen.

7. The string 25/5+2 will be displayed on the screen.

8. Move the cursor to the G in PRING with the left arrow key found just below the number 4 on the right side of the keyboard. Then type in a T and press the ENTER key.

Chapter 3

1. Press the ENTER key.

2. While holding down the Ctrl key, press the Break key (found on the front face of the key marked Scr Lock). Recall that this is referred to as Ctrl-Break.

3. Press Ctrl-Break.

4. The statement **PRINT C** has no line number.

5. The number 2 would be displayed on the screen.

6. Up to 40 characters.

7. Type the line using a line number not already in the program.

8. Retype the line including the line number.

9. Type the line number and press the ENTER key.

10. Type LIST and press ENTER.

11. Type CLS and press ENTER.

12. Type RUN and press ENTER.

13. Type NEW and press ENTER.

14. A character string variable always ends with a $.

15. Displays line 120 for editing with the left arrow, right arrow, Del and Ins keys.

Chapter 4

1. A square.

2. A house.

3. **DRAW "BM160,100 R80 U40 L40 D40"**

4. a. PSET (160,100) b. PSET (0,0) c. PSET (160,0) d. PSET (240,150)

5. a. 30 b. (140,90)

6. **CIRCLE(80,50),40,1**

7. **a.** If you have only the IBM Monochrome Display Monitor, you cannot access the graphics mode. If you have only the Color/Graphics Display Adapter, type in **SCREEN 1**. If you have both, see Appendix A.
   b. Enter a **SCREEN 1,0**.

8. A4

9. C2, the second note

Chapter 5

1. **a.** * **b.** ^ **c.** /

2. **a.** Exponentiation **b.** Multiplication and division **c.** Addition and subtraction

3. Left to right.

4. **100 LET A = (4+3*B/D)^2**

5. 4

6. **a.** 5.16E+06 **b.** 3.14E-05

7. **a.** 7258000 **b.** 0.001437

8. / then + then ^

9. **a.** Type **LOAD"** (name of program) and press ENTER.
   b. Type **SAVE"** (name of program) and press ENTER.
   c. Type **KILL"** (name of program) and press ENTER.
   d. Type **NEW** and press ENTER.
   e. Type **LIST** and press ENTER.
   f. Type **RUN** and press ENTER.
   g. Type **FILES** and press ENTER.

10. Use the left arrow key under the number 4 on the right side of the keyboard to move the cursor to the error and type the correct character. Then press ENTER.

Chapter 6

1.
```
1  2  3  4  5  6
7  8  9  10 11 12
13 14 15 16 17 18
19 20 21 22 23 24
etc.
```

2. **a.** By assignment (e.g., **100 LET A = 3**) **b.** INPUT statements **c.** READ and DATA statements

3. A string.

4. To provide information within the program for the benefit of the programmer or user.

5. DATA.

6. Y = 3 will be printed out.

7. Six (for an 80 column screen).

8. As many as needed.

9. To provide a method to obtain variable spacing in the output.

10.
```
1             3
1 3
```

11.
```
?10,12,13
Redo from start
?
```

2.
```
100 PRINT "INPUT NO. OF MILES";
110 INPUT N
120 LET K = 1.609*N
130 PRINT N;" MILES EQUALS ";K
140 PRINT "KILOMETERS"
150 END
```

Chapter 7

1.
```
6
10
14
18
```

2.
```
BEST

BETTER
BEST

GOOD
BETTER
BEST

OUT OF DATA IN LINE 100
```

3.
```
100 PRINT "HOW MANY WIDGETS";
110 INPUT N
120 IF N <= 20 THEN 160
130 IF N <= 50 THEN 180
140 LET U = 1.5
150 GOTO 190
160 LET U = 2
170 GOTO 190
180 LET U = 1.8
190 LET P = N*U
200 PRINT "PRICE PER WIDGET IS ";U
210 PRINT "TOTAL COST OF ORDER IS";P
220 PRINT
230 GOTO 100
240 END
```

4.
```
100 LET X = 0
110 PRINT X,
120 LET X = X+5
130 IF X <= 175 THEN 110
140 END
```

5.
```
100 PRINT "WHAT WAS SPEED LIMIT ";
110 INPUT A
120 PRINT "SPEED ARRESTED AT ";
130 INPUT B
140 LET X = B-A
150 IF X <= 10 THEM 210
160 IF X <= 20 THEN 230
170 IF X <= 30 THEN 250
180 IF X <= 40 THEN 270
190 LET F = 80
200 GOTO 280
210 LET F = 5
220 GOTO 280
230 LET F = 10
240 GOTO 280
250 LET F = 20
260 GOTO 280
270 LET F = 40
280 PRINT "FINE IS ";F;" DOLLARS"
290 END
```

Chapter 8

1.
```
20 18 16 14 12 10
8  6  4  2
```

2.
```
1 2 3 2 4 6
3 6 9 4 8 12
```

3. **a.** 6 **b.** 7 **c.** 22.8 **d.** -1

4. The loops are crossed.

5.
```
100 PRINT "MILES","KILOMETERS"
110 PRINT "-----","----------"
120 PRINT
130 FOR M = 10 TO 100 STEP 5
140 PRINT M,1.609*M
150 NEXT M
160 END
```

6.
```
100 DATA 10
110 DATA 25,21,24,21,26,27,25,24,23,24
120 READ N
130 LET S = 0
140 FOR I = 1 TO N
150 READ X
160 LET S = S+X
170 NEXT I
180 PRINT S/N
190 END
```

7. Six.

Chapter 9

1. To save space for an array.

2. X(3,4)

3.
```
100 DIM A(50)
110 PRINT "HOW MANY NUMBERS ";
120 INPUT N
130 PRINT "WHAT ARE THE NUMBERS";
140 FOR I = 1 TO N
150 INPUT A(I)
160 NEXT I
170 LET S = 0
180 FOR I = 1 TO N
190 IF A(I) <= 0 THEN 210
200 LET S = S+A(I)
210 NEXT I
220 PRINT "SUM OF POSITIVE ELEMENTS IS ";S
230 END
```

4.
```
100 FOR R = 1 TO 4
110 FOR C = 1 TO 6
120 LET X(R,C) = 4
130 NEXT C
140 NEXT R
150 END
```

5.
```
2 0 0 0 0
0 2 0 0 0
0 0 2 0 0
0 0 0 2 0
0 0 0 0 2
```

6. **a.** `100 DIM A(2,3)` **b.** A(2,3) = 4 **c.** A(X,Y) = A(1,2) = 3
d. A(A(1,1), A(2,2)) = A(1,2) = 4

Chapter 10

1. By appending $ to a numeric variable name.

2. False

3. `MID$(A$,5,9)`

4.
```
100 INPUT A$
110 FOR X = LEN(A$) TO 1 STEP 1
120 PRINT MID$(A$,1,X)
130 NEXT X
140 END
```

5.
```
a
ab
abc
abcd
abcde

    etc.

abcdefghijklmnopqrstuvwxyz
```

Chapter 11

a. 4 **b.** 14 **c.** 30 **d.** 80

```
2 1 3
4
```

a. Type in **GOSUB** (line number at beginning of subroutine)
b. **RETURN**

```
WHITE
RED
BLUE
```

Chapter 12

```
60 LET Y$ = TIME$
70 LET A$ = MID$(Y$,7,2)
80 LET N = VAL(A$)
90 RANDOMIZE(N)
100 FOR I = 1 TO 100
110 LET X = INT(4*RND+1)
120 PRINT X,
130 NEXT I
140 END
```

```
60 LET Y$ = TIME$
70 LET A$ = MID$(Y$,7,2)
80 LET N = VAL(A$)
90 RANDOMIZE(N)
100 FOR I = 1 TO 100
110 LET X = 25+25*RND
120 PRINT X,
130 NEXT I
140 END
```

3. The output will be randomly selected from WHITE and RED. Three program outputs are shown to indicate the random nature of the process.

(1)	(2)	(3)
RED	WHITE	WHITE
RED	WHITE	RED
WHITE	RED	WHITE
WHITE	WHITE	WHITE
RED	WHITE	WHITE
RED	RED	WHITE
RED	RED	RED
WHITE	RED	WHITE
RED	WHITE	WHITE
RED	WHITE	RED

4. Five random numbers of the form X.XX over the range 0.00 to 9.99. Three program outputs are shown below to illustrate the random nature of the process.

(1)	(2)	(3)
0.51	6.69	1.15
9.34	4.04	8.87
9.08	9.06	9.26
9.26	6.71	2.59
5.98	8.15	3.05

SOLUTION TO ODD-NUMBERED PROBLEMS

Chapter 6

1.
```
100 REM CHAP 6, PROB 1
110 READ A,B,C,D
120 DATA 10,9,1,2
130 LET S = A+B
140 LET P = C*D
150 PRINT S,P
160 END
```

3.
```
100 REM CHAP 6, PROB 3
110 READ A,B,C,D
120 DATA 21,18,6,3
130 PRINT A
140 PRINT B
150 PRINT C
160 PRINT D
170 END
```

5. There is no value assigned to C.

7.
```
100 REM CHAP 6, PROB 7
110 PRINT "CASH = ";
120 INPUT C
130 PRINT "MARKETABLE SECURITIES = ";
140 INPUT M
150 PRINT "RECEIVABLES =";
160 INPUT R
170 PRINT "LIABILITIES = ";
180 INPUT L
190 LET A = (C+M+R)/L
200 PRINT "ACID-TEST RATIO = ";A
210 END
```

9. The program loops back to line 100 where A is set equal to 1 after each printout. The program can be corrected by changing line 130 as follows.

```
130 GOTO 110
```

11. The problem lies in statements 100, 110, and 120. The values of L, W, and H are supposed to be printed out, but they haven't been defined. The computer will assign the value zero to the three variables and these zeros are printed out by lines 100, 110, 120. The program may be corrected by deleting line 130 and L, W, and H at the ends of lines 100, 110, and 120. Now, the following lines need to be added.

```
105 INPUT L
115 INPUT W
125 INPUT H
```

14.
```
100 REM CHAP 6, PROB 13
110 DATA 21423,21493,5
120 DATA 5270,5504,13
130 DATA 65214,65559,11.5
140 READ R1,R2,G
150 LET M = (R2-R1)/G
160 PRINT M
170 GOTO 140
180 END
```

16.
```
100 REM CHAP 6, PROB 15
110 DATA 92,63,75,82,72,53,100,89,70,81
120 READ A,B,C,D,E,F,G,H,I,J
130 PRINT (A+B+C+D+E+F+G+H+I+J)/10
140 END
```

18.
```
100 REM CHAP 6, PROB 17
110 PRINT "QUOTED INTEREST RATE (PERCENT) "
120 INPUT R
130 PRINT "NUMBER OF TIMES COMPOUNDED PER YEAR "
140 INPUT M
150 LET T = ((1+R/(100*M))^M-1)*100
160 PRINT "TRUE ANNUAL INTEREST RATE IS"
170 PRINT T
180 END
```

19.
```
100 REM CHAP 6, PROB 19
110 PRINT "INITIAL INVESTMENT ";
120 INPUT P
130 PRINT "ANNUAL INTEREST RATE(%) ";
140 INPUT I
150 PRINT "YEARS LEFT TO ACCRUE INTEREST ";
160 INPUT N
170 LET T = P*(1+I/100)^N
180 PRINT "TOTAL VALUE IS ";T
190 END
```

Chapter 7

1.
```
100 REM CHAP 7, PROB 1
110 INPUT X,Y
120 IF X>Y THEN 150
130 PRINT Y
140 GOTO 160
150 PRINT X
160 END
```

3.
```
100 REM CHAP 7, PROB 3
110 LET S = 0
120 LET X = 1
130 LET S = S+X
140 LET X = X+1
150 IF X <= 100 THEN 130
160 PRINT S
170 END
```

5.
```
OUT OF DATA IN LINE 120
```

7.
```
100 REM CHAP 7, PROB 7
110 LET S = 0
120 READ X
130 IF X = 9999 THEN 180
140 IF X<-10 THEN 120
150 IF X>10 THEN 120
160 LET S = S+X
170 GOTO 120
180 PRINT S
190 DATA -1,22,17,-6,4,7,9999
200 END
```

9.
```
100 REM CHAP 7, PROB 9
110 LET C = 1
120 LET T = 0
130 LET W = 1
140 LET T = T+W
150 LET C = C+1
160 LET W = 2*W
170 IF C <= 22 THEN 140
180 PRINT W/100
190 END
```

11. The number 83 will be printed out. The program finds the largest number contained in the two DATA statements.

13.
```
100 REM CHAP 7, PROB 13
110 PRINT "LIST PRICE ($) ";
120 INPUT L
130 PRINT "DISCOUNT RATE (%) ";
140 INPUT R
150 LET D = L*(1 - R/100)
160 PRINT "DISCOUNTED PRICE IS"
170 PRINT D;" DOLLARS"
180 END
```

15.
```
100 REM CHAP 7, PROB 15
110 INPUT A,B
120 IF A >= 10 THEN 130
121 GOTO 150
130 IF B >= 10 THEN 140
131 GOTO 150
140 PRINT A+B
141 GOTO 210
150 IF A < 10 THEN 160
151 GOTO 180
160 IF B < 10 THEN 170
161 GOTO 180
170 PRINT A*B
171 GOTO 210
180 IF A < B THEN 200
```

```
190 PRINT A-B
191 GOTO 210
200 PRINT B-A
210 END
```

17.

```
100 REM CHAP 7, PROB 17
110 PRINT "GROWTH RATE (%) ";
120 INPUT R
130 LET N = 0
140 LET Q = 1
150 LET Q = Q*(1+R/100)
160 LET N = N+1
170 IF Q <= 2 THEN 150
180 PRINT "NUMBER OF GROWTH PERIODS TO DOUBLE IS ";N
190 END
```

19.

```
100 REM CHAP 7, PROB 19
110 LET A$ = INKEY$
120 IF A$ = "U" THEN DRAW "U10"
130 IF A$ = "D" THEN DRAW "D10"
140 IF A$ = "L" THEN DRAW "L10"
150 IF A$ = "R" THEN DRAW "R10"
160 IF A$ = "Q" THEN END ELSE 110
```

Chapter 8

1.

```
100 REM CHAP 8, PROB 1
110 PRINT "N","SQR(N)"
120 PRINT
130 FOR N = 2 TO 4 STEP .1
140 PRINT N,SQR(N)
150 NEXT N
160 END
```

3.

```
100 REM CHAP 8, PROB 3
110 INPUT N
120 FOR X = 2 TO N STEP 2
130 PRINT X
140 NEXT X
150 END
```

5.
```
         ABCDEFGHIJ
        ABCDEFGHIJ
       ABCDEFGHIJ
      ABCDEFGHIJ
     ABCDEFGHIJ
    ABCDEFGHIJ
   ABCDEFGHIJ
  ABCDEFGHIJ
 ABCDEFGHIJ
ABCDEFGHIJ
```

7. Since the Z and V loops are crossed, an error message will appear.

9. It reads and prints out five numbers rounded off to two places past the decimal point.

11.
```
100 REM CHAP 8, PROB 11
110 FOR I = 40 TO 220 STEP 60
120 PLAY "T = I;"
130 PLAY "C4D4E4C4 P8 C4D4E4C4"
140 PLAY "P8 E4F4G4 P4 E4F4G4"
150 PLAY "P4 G8A8G8F8 P32 E8C2"
160 PLAY "P4 G8A8G8F8 P32 E8C2"
170 PLAY "P4 C4 O3G4 O4C4 P6 C4 O3G4 O4C4"
180 NEXT I
190 END
```

13.
```
100 REM CHAP 8, PROB 13
110 INPUT N
120 INPUT X
130 LET L = X
140 LET H = X
150 LET S = 0
160 FOR I = 1 TO N-1
170 INPUT X
180 IF X > L THEN 200
190 LET L = X
200 IF X < H THEN 220
210 LET H = X
220 LET S = S+X
230 NEXT I
```

```
240 PRINT "HIGHEST GRADE IS ";H
250 PRINT "LOWEST GRADE IS ";L
260 PRINT "AVERAGE IS ";S/N
270 END
```

```
1 2 3
2 4 6
3 6 9
4 8 12
```

```
100 REM CHAP 8, PROB 17
110 READ N
120 FOR I = 1 TO N
130 READ M,R,D1,D2,D3,D4,D5
140 PRINT "EMPLOYEE NUMBER ";M
150 LET H = D1+D2+D3+D4+D5
160 IF H <= 40 THEN 180
170 LET P = R*40 + 1.5*R*(H-40)
175 GOTO 185
180 LET P = R*H
185 PRINT "PAY IS ";P
190 DATA 5
200 DATA 2,4.8,8,10,8,7,10
201 DATA 5,3.75,7,8,8,6,10
202 DATA 1,3.25,8,10,6,8,8
203 DATA 4,5,8,10,6,10,6
204 DATA 3,4.25,6,6,8,10,7
210 END
```

Chapter 9

```
100 REM CHAP 9, PROB 1
110 DIM X(20)
120 READ N
130 FOR I = 1 TO N
150 READ X(I)
160 NEXT I
170 FOR I = 1 TO N
180 PRINT X(I)
190 NEXT I
200 DATA 12
210 DATA 2,1,4,3,2,4,5,6,3,5,4,1
220 END
```

3.
```
100 REM CHAP 9, PROB 3
110 DIM A(10,10)
120 INPUT N
130 FOR R = 1 TO N
140 FOR C = 1 TO N
150 INPUT A(R,C)
160 NEXT C
170 NEXT R
180 LET S = 0
190 FOR I = 1 TO N
200 LET S = S + A(I,I)
210 NEXT I
220 PRINT "SUM OF MAIN DIAGONAL IS ";S
230 END
```

5.
```
100 REM CHAP 9, PROB 5
110 DIM A(15,15)
120 INPUT M,N
130 FOR R = 1 TO M
140 FOR C = 1 TO N
150 INPUT A(R,C)
160 NEXT C
170 NEXT R
180 LET S = 0
190 FOR R = 1 TO M
200 FOR C = 1 TO N
210 LET S = S+A(R,C)
220 NEXT C
230 NEXT R
240 PRINT "SUM OF ENTRIES IS ";S
250 END
```

7. 10

9. 16

11.
```
100 REM CHAP 9, PROB 11
110 DIM X(100)
120 INPUT N
130 FOR I = 1 TO N
140 INPUT X(I)
```

```
150 NEXT I
160 FOR I = 1 TO N-1
170 IF X(I-1)<X(I) THEN 220
180 LET T = X(I+1)
190 LET X(I+1) = X(I)
200 LET X(I) = T
210 GOTO 140
220 NEXT I
230 FOR I = 1 TO N
240 PRINT X(I);
250 NEXT I
260 END
```

.

```
1 1 1 1 1 1
0 0 0 0 0 0
0 0 1 1 1 1
0 0 0 0 0 0
0 0 0 0 1 1
0 0 0 0 0 0
```

5.

```
100 REM CHAP 9, PROB 15
110 DIM X(2,5)
120 FOR R = 1 TO 2
130 FOR C = 1 TO 5
140 READ X(R,C)
150 NEXT C
160 NEXT R
170 DATA 2,1,0,5,1
180 DATA 3,2,1,3,1
190 FOR R = 1 TO 2
200 FOR C = 1 TO 5
210 PRINT X(R,C),
220 NEXT C
230 PRINT
240 NEXT R
250 END
```

7.

```
100 REM CHAP 9, PROB 17
110 DIM X(20,20)
120 INPUT M,N
130 FOR R = 1 TO M
```

```
140 FOR C = 1 TO N
150 INPUT X(R,C)
160 NEXT C
170 NEXT R
180 FOR R = 1 TO M
190 LET S = 0
200 FOR C = 1 TO N
210 LET S = S+X(R,C)
220 NEXT C
230 PRINT "SUM OF ROW ";R;" IS ";S
240 NEXT R
250 FOR C = 1 TO N
260 LET P = 1
270 FOR R = 1 TO M
280 LET P = P*X(R,C)
290 NEXT R
300 PRINT "PRODUCT OF COLUMN ";C;" IS ";P
310 NEXT C
320 END
```

19.

```
100 REM CHAP 9, PROB 19
110 DIM X(4,6)
120 FOR R = 1 TO 4
130 FOR C = 1 TO 6
140 READ X(R,C)
150 NEXT C
160 NEXT R
170 DATA 48,40,73,120,100,90
180 DATA 75,130,90,140,110,85
190 DATA 50,72,140,125,106,92
200 DATA 108,75,92,152,91,87
210 FOR C = 1 TO 6
220 LET S = 0
230 FOR R = 1 TO 4
240 LET S = S+X(R,C)
250 NEXT R
260 PRINT "TOTAL-DAY ";C;" IS ";S
270 NEXT C
285 PRINT
290 FOR R = 1 TO 4
300 LET S = 0
```

```
310 FOR C = 1 TO 6
320 LET S = S+X(R,C)
330 NEXT C
340 PRINT "TOTAL-SALESPERSON ";R;" IS ";S
350 NEXT R
360 LET S = 0
370 FOR R = 1 TO 4
380 FOR C = 1 TO 6
390 LET S = S+X(R,C)
400 NEXT C
410 NEXT R
420 PRINT
430 PRINT "TOTAL SALES FOR THE WEEK IS ";S
440 END
```

```
100 REM CHAP 9, PROB 21
110 DIM P(20),X(20)
120 PRINT "HOW LONG ARE THE ARRAYS ";
130 INPUT N
140 FOR I = 1 TO N
150 LET P(I) = I
160 NEXT I
170 FOR R = 1 TO N
180 INPUT X(R)
190 NEXT R
200 FOR I = 1 TO N-1
210 IF X(P(I))>X(P(I+1)) THEN 240
220 LET T = P(I)
230 LET P(I) = P(I+1)
240 LET P(I+1) = T
250 GOTO 180
260 NEXT I
270 PRINT "P","X"
280 PRINT
290 FOR I = 1 TO N
300 PRINT P(I),X(I)
310 NEXT I
320 END
```

Chapter 10

1.
```
100 REM CHAP 10, PROB 1
110 INPUT A$
120 FOR I = 1 TO LEN(A$)
130 PRINT MID$(A$,I,1)
140 NEXT I
150 END
```

3.
```
100 REM CHAP 10, PROB 3
110 INPUT A$
120 LET A = 0
130 LET E = 0
140 LET I = 0
150 LET O = 0
160 LET U = 0
170 FOR I = I TO LEN(A$)
180 IF MID$(A$,I,1) = "A" THEN 240
190 IF MID$(A$,I,1) = "E" THEN 260
200 IF MID$(A$,I,1) = "I" THEN 280
210 IF MID$(A$,I,1) = "O" THEN 300
220 IF MID$(A$,I,1) = "U" THEN 320
230 GOTO 340
240 LET A = A+1
250 GOTO 340
260 LET E = E+1
270 GOTO 340
280 LET I = I+1
290 GOTO 340
300 LET O = O+1
310 GOTO 340
320 LET U = U+1
330 NEXT I
360 PRINT "A = ";A
370 PRINT "E = ";E
380 PRINT "I = ";I
390 PRINT "O = ";O
380 PRINT "U = ";U
390 END
```

```
100 REM CHAP 10, PROB 5
110 INPUT A$
120 LET J = 1
130 FOR I = 1 TO LEN(A$)
140 IF MID$(A$,I,1) = CHR$(32) THEN 170
150 LET MID$(B$,J,1) = MID$(A$,I,1)
160 LET J = J+1
170 NEXT I
180 PRINT B$
190 END
```

```
100 REM CHAP 10, PROB 7
110 LET C = 0
120 FOR K = 1 TO 5
130 INPUT A$
140 IF MID$(A$,1,4)<>"THE " THEN 160
150 LET C = C+1
160 FOR I = 2 TO LEN(A$)-3
170 IF MID$(A$,I,4)<>"THE " THEN 190
180 LET C = C+1
190 NEXT I
200 PRINT C
210 END
```

```
100 REM CHAP 10, PROB 9
110 INPUT A$
120 LET C = 0
130 FOR K = 1 TO LEN(A$)-1
140 IF MID$(A$,K,2)<>"IN" THEN 160
150 LET C = C+1
160 NEXT K
170 PRINT C
180 END
```

Chapter 11

```
25 5 20
65
```

3.
```
100 REM CHAP 11, PROB 3
110 DEF FNA(R) = 3.14159*R^2
120 DEF FNB(R) = 4*3.14159*R^3/3
130 PRINT
140 PRINT "R","AREA OF","VOLUME OF"
150 PRINT " ","CIRCLE","SPHERE"
160 PRINT
170 FOR R = 1 TO 10 STEP .5
180 PRINT R,FNA(R),FNB(R)
190 NEXT R
200 END
```

5.
```
55
15
91
```

7.
```
500 REM SUBROUTINE
510 LET L = X(2)
520 FOR I = 2 TO X(1)
530 IF L >= X(I) THEN 550
540 LET L = X(I)
550 NEXT I
560 RETURN
```

9.
```
900 REM SUBROUTINE
910 LET S1 = 0
920 LET S2 = 0
930 FOR I = 2 TO Y(1)+1
940 LET S1 = S1+Y(I)
950 LET S2 = S2+Y(I)^2
960 NEXT I
970 LET M = S1/Y(1)
980 LET S = SQR((Y(1)*S2-S1^2)/(Y(1)*(Y(1)-1)))
990 RETURN
```

Chapter 12

1.
```
50 REM CHAP 12, PROB 1
60 LET Y$ = TIME$
70 LET A$ = MID$(Y$,7,2)
80 LET N = VAL(A$)
90 RANDOMIZE(N)
```

```
100 FOR I = 1 TO 25
110 LET N = INT(100*RND)/10
120 PRINT N,
130 NEXT I
140 END
```

A typical output is:

```
.04 .02 .17 .14 .01
.03 .16 .04 .05 .17
.19 .12 .07 .11 .19
.11 .19 .2  .18 .04
```

```
50 REM CHAP 12, PROB 5
60 LET Y$= TIME$
70 LET A$= MID$(Y$,7,2)
80 LET N = VAL(A$)
90 RANDOMIZE(N)
100 FOR I = 1 TO 5
110 READ N
120 LET H = 0
130 LET T = 0
140 FOR J = 1 TO N
150 LET X = INT(2*RND+1)
160 IF X = 1 THEN 190
170 LET T = T+1
180 GOTO 200
190 LET H = H+1
200 NEXT J
210 PRINT
220 PRINT "FOR ";N;" TOSSES THERE WERE"
230 PRINT H;" HEADS AND ";T;" TAILS"
240 NEXT I
250 DATA 10,50,100,500,1000
260 END
```

```
50 REM CHAP 12, PROB 7
60 LET Y$= TIME$
70 LET A$= MID$(Y$,7,2)
80 LET N = VAL(A$)
90 RANDOMIZE(N)
```

```
100 LET S = 0
110 FOR I = 1 TO 1000
120 LET S = S+RND
130 NEXT I
140 PRINT S/1000
150 END
```

9.
```
50 REM CHAP 12, PROB 9
60 LET Y$= TIME$
70 LET A$= MID$(Y$,7,2)
80 LET N = VAL(A$)
90 RANDOMIZE(N)
100 LET M = 0
110 FOR I = 1 TO 1000
120 LET A = 60*RND
130 LET B = 60*RND
140 IF ABS(A-B)>10 THEN 160
150 LET M = M+1
160 NEXT I
170 PRINT "PROBABILITY OF A MEET IS ";M/1000
180 END
```

11.
```
50 REM CHAP 12, PROB 11
60 LET Y$= TIME$
70 LET A$= MID$(Y$,7,2)
80 LET N = VAL(A$)
90 RANDOMIZE(N)
100 FOR I = 1 TO 25
110 LET S = 0
120 FOR J = 1 TO 12
130 LET S = S+RND(0)
140 NEXT J
150 LET R = 10+2*(S-6)
160 PRINT INT(100*R+.5)/100,
170 NEXT I
180 END
```

INDEX

9780070491786